THE BOOKS OF ENOCH
COMPLETE EDITION

Paul C. Schnieders

INCLUDING

ENOCH 1 – THE ETHIOPIAN BOOK OF ENOCH

ENOCH 2 – THE SLAVONIC SECRETS OF ENOCH

ENOCH 3 – THE HEBREW BOOK OF ENOCH

Translated by R.H. Charles

International Alliance Pro-Publishing © 2012

Printed in the United States.

ISBN: 978-1-60942-200-4

Schnieders, Paul C.

The Books of Enoch: Complete Edition. Paul C. Schnieders − 1st ed.

1. Religion.

Table of Contents

The Book of Enoch

Section 1: Chapters 1-36

Enoch's journeys and vision, and the fallen angels

Section 2: Chapters 37-71

The Parables

Section 3: Chapters 72-82

The Book of the Heavenly Luminaries

Section 4: Chapters 83-90

The Dream-Visions

Section 5: Chapters 91- 104

A Book of Exhortation and Promised Blessing for the Righteous and of Malediction and Woe for the Sinners

The Book of the Secrets of Enoch

Hebrew Book of Enoch

INTRODUCTION

In the Bible, Enoch is the name of four persons. The first is the oldest son of Cain (Gen. 4:17); the second, the son of Jared (Gen. 5:18); the third, the son of Midian (Gen. 25:4); the fourth, the oldest son of Reuben (Gen. 46:9; Ex. 6:14).

The Book of Enoch is an old composition considered a pseudoepigraphal work (a work that claims to be by a biblical character). It is also considered an apocryphal work meaning it has a hidden or unknown origin or it is known only in private circles. It was included with other apocryphal books in the Ethiopic Bible, which was composed by Syrian monks who had come to Ethiopia in the 5th century fleeing a Byzantine persecution. Nearly all of the church Fathers knew of an apocryphal Book of Enoch, and their description of the work and citations from it prove satisfactorily that it was virtually the same as that which now lies before us. According to some of them, such as Irenaeus, Tertullian etc. the Book of Enoch (1 Enoch) was rejected by the Jews and left out of the Jewish bible canon because it contained prophecies about Christ. By the 4th century, it was excluded from the canon by most of the Christian church. Still today it's included in the biblical canon of the Ethiopian Orthodox Church and the Eritrean Orthodox Church.

Among the apocryphal works one kind is embraced under the term apocalyptic. This latter class is of a prophetic character, and under the assumption of a super human source of information seeks to unravel the mysteries of the present and the future. The Book of Enoch is in this class.

Two versions were called books of Enoch - an Ethiopic one (translated from Ethiopic) called '1 Enoch', by scholars and a Slavonic version identified as '2 Enoch', which is also known as *The Book of the Secrets of Enoch*.

The discovery of the texts from Qumran Cave 4 has finally provided parts of the Aramaic original (Ethiopic version) of the Book of Enoch. Paleographic dating of the Enoch fragments found (4Q201) revealed it was copied around 200-150 BC. The first Ethiopic version published in the West was printed in the 19th century.

1 Enoch is referred in Jude 14-15 and also in I Peter 3:19, 20 to En. 21:6.

Concerning *2 Enoch,* it preserved solely in the Slavonic language. This version was rediscovered and printed in the 19th century. It has survived in about twenty manuscripts and fragments in Slavonic, copied from the 14th to the 18th century.

Paul C. Schnieders

The Book of Enoch

Section 1

Chapters 1-36

Enoch's journeys and vision,
and the fallen angels

Chapters 1-5

*Parable of Enoch on the Future Lot
of the Wicked and the Righteous*

CHAPTER 1

[1]The words of the blessing of Enoch, wherewith he blessed the elect and righteous, who will be [2]living in the day of tribulation, when all the wicked and godless are to be removed. And he took up his parable and said –Enoch a righteous man, whose eyes were opened by God, saw the vision of the Holy One in the heavens, which the angels showed me, and from them I heard everything, and from them I understood as I saw, but not for this generation, but for a remote one which is [3]for to come. Concerning the elect I said, and took up my parable concerning them:

The Holy Great One will come forth from His dwelling,

[4]And the eternal God will tread upon the earth, (even) on Mount Sinai,
[And appear from His camp]
And appear in the strength of His might from the heaven of heavens.

[5]And all shall be smitten with fear
And the Watchers shall quake,
And great fear and trembling shall seize them unto the ends of the earth.

[6]And the high mountains shall be shaken,
And the high hills shall be made low,
And shall melt like wax before the flame.

[7]And the earth shall be wholly rent in sunder,
And all that is upon the earth shall perish,
And there shall be a judgment upon all (men).

[8]But with the righteous He will make peace,
And will protect the elect,
And mercy shall be upon them.

And they shall all belong to God,
And they shall be prospered,
And they shall all be blessed.

And He will help them all,

And light shall appear unto them,
And He will make peace with them.

[9]And behold! He cometh with ten thousands of His holy ones
To execute judgment upon all,
And to destroy all the ungodly:

And to convict all flesh
Of all the works of their ungodliness which they have ungodly committed,
And of all the hard things which ungodly sinners have spoken against Him.

CHAPTER 2

[1]Observe ye everything that takes place in the heaven, how they do not change their orbits, and the luminaries which are in the heaven, how they all rise and set in order each in its season, and [2]transgress not against their appointed order. Behold ye the earth, and give heed to the things which take place upon it from first to last, how steadfast they are, how none of the things upon earth [3]change, but all the works of God appear to you. Behold the summer and the winter, how the whole earth is filled with water, and clouds and dew and rain lie upon it.

CHAPTER 3

Observe and see how (in the winter) all the trees seem as though they had withered and shed all their leaves, except fourteen trees, which do not lose their foliage but retain the old foliage from two to three years till the new comes.

CHAPTER 4

And again, observe ye the days of summer how the sun is above the earth over against it. And you seek shade and shelter by reason of the heat of the sun, and the earth also burns with glowing heat, and so you cannot tread on the earth, or on a rock by reason of its heat.

CHAPTER 5

[1]Observe ye how the trees cover themselves with green leaves and bear fruit: wherefore give ye heed and know with regard to all His works, and recognize how He that liveth for ever hath made them so. [2]And all His works go on thus from year to year for ever, and all the tasks which they accomplish for Him, and their tasks change not, but according as God hath ordained so is it done. [3]And behold how the sea and the rivers in like manner accomplish and change not their tasks from His commandments'.

[4]But ye —ye have not been steadfast, nor done the commandments of the Lord,
But ye have turned away and spoken proud and hard words
With your impure mouths against His greatness.
Oh, ye hardhearted, ye shall find no peace.

[5]Therefore shall ye execrate your days,
And the years of your life shall perish,
And the years of your destruction shall be multiplied in eternal execration,
And ye shall find no mercy.

[6a]In those days ye shall make your names an eternal execration unto all the righteous,

[b]And by you shall all who curse, curse,
And all the sinners and godless shall imprecate by you,

[7c]And for you the godless there shall be a curse.

[6d]And all the ... shall rejoice,

[e]And there shall be forgiveness of sins,

[f]And every mercy and peace and forbearance:

[g]There shall be salvation unto them, a goodly light.

[h]And for all of you sinners there shall be no salvation,

[i]But on you all shall abide a curse.

[7a]But for the elect there shall be light and joy and peace,

[b]And they shall inherit the earth.

[8]And then there shall be bestowed upon the elect wisdom,
And they shall all live and never again sin,
Either through ungodliness or through pride:
But they who are wise shall be humble.

[9]And they shall not again transgress,
Nor shall they sin all the days of their life,
Nor shall they die of (the divine) anger or wrath,
But they shall complete the number of the days of their life.
And their lives shall be increased in peace,
And the years of their joy shall be multiplied,
In eternal gladness and peace,
All the days of their life.

Chapters 6-11

*The Fall of the Angels: the Demoralization of Mankind: the
Intercession of the Angels on behalf of Mankind. The Dooms
pronounced by God on the Angels of the Messianic
Kingdom—(a Noah fragment)*

CHAPTER 6

[1]And it came to pass when the children of men had multiplied that in those days were born unto [2]them beautiful and comely daughters. And the angels, the children of the heaven, saw and lusted after them, and said to one another: 'Come, let us choose us wives from among the children of men [3]and beget us children.' And Semjâzâ, who was their leader, said unto them: 'I fear ye will not [4]indeed agree to do this deed, and I alone shall have to pay the penalty of a great sin.' And they all answered him and said: 'Let us all swear an oath, and all bind ourselves by mutual imprecations [5]not to abandon this plan but to do this thing.' Then sware they all together and bound themselves [6]by mutual imprecations upon it. And they were in all two hundred; who descended in the days of Jared on the summit of Mount Hermon, and they called it Mount Hermon, because they had sworn [7]and bound themselves by mutual imprecations upon it. And these are the names of their leaders: Samîazâz, their leader, Arâkîba, Râmêêl, Kôkabîêl, Tâmîêl, Râmîêl, Dânêl, Êzêqêêl, Barâqîjâl, [8]Asâêl, Armârôs, Batârêl, Anânêl, Zaqîêl, Samsâpêêl, Satarêl, Tûrêl, Jômjâêl, Sariêl. These are their chiefs of tens.

CHAPTER 7

[1]And all the others together with them took unto themselves wives, and each chose for himself one, and they began to go in unto them and to defile themselves with them, and they taught them charms [2]and enchantments, and the cutting of roots, and made them acquainted with plants. And they [3]became pregnant, and they bare great giants, whose height was three thousand ells: Who consumed [4]all the acquisitions of men. And when men could no longer sustain them, the giants turned against [5]them and devoured mankind. And they began to sin against birds, and beasts, and reptiles, and [6]fish, and to devour one another's flesh, and drink the blood. Then the earth laid accusation against the lawless ones.

CHAPTER 8

[1]And Azâzêl taught men to make swords, and knives, and shields, and breastplates, and made known to them the metals of the earth and the art of working them, and bracelets, and ornaments, and the use of antimony, and the beautifying of the eyelids, and all kinds of costly stones, and all [2]colouring tinctures. And there arose much godlessness, and they committed fornication, and they [3]were led astray, and became corrupt in all their ways. Semjâzâ taught enchantments, and root-cuttings, 'Armârôs the resolving of enchantments, Barâqîjâl (taught) astrology, Kôkabêl the constellations, Êzêqêêl the knowledge of the clouds, Araqiêl the signs of the earth, Shamsiêl the signs of the sun, and Sariêl the course of the moon. And as men perished, they cried, and their cry went up to heaven...

CHAPTER 9

[1]And then Michael, Uriel, Raphael, and Gabriel looked down from heaven and saw much blood being [2]shed upon the earth, and all lawlessness being wrought upon the earth. And they said one to another: 'The earth made without inhabitant cries the voice of their cryingst up to the gates of heaven. [3]And now to you, the holy ones of heaven, the souls of men make their suit, saying, "Bring our cause [4]before the Most High." And they said to the Lord of the ages: 'Lord of lords, God of gods, King of kings, and God of the ages, the throne of Thy glory (standeth) unto all the generations of the [5]ages, and Thy name holy and glorious and blessed unto all the ages! Thou hast made all

things, and power over all things hast Thou: and all things are naked and open in Thy sight, and Thou seest all [6]things, and nothing can hide itself from Thee. Thou seest what Azâzêl hath done, who hath taught all unrighteousness on earth and revealed the eternal secrets which were (preserved) in heaven, which [7]men were striving to learn: And Semjâzâ, to whom Thou hast given authority to bear rule over his associates. And they have gone to the daughters of men upon the earth, and have slept with the [9]women, and have defiled themselves, and revealed to them all kinds of sins. And the women have [10]borne giants, and the whole earth has thereby been filled with blood and unrighteousness. And now, behold, the souls of those who have died are crying and making their suit to the gates of heaven, and their lamentations have ascended: and cannot cease because of the lawless deeds which are [11]wrought on the earth. And Thou knowest all things before they come to pass, and Thou seest these things and Thou dost suffer them, and Thou dost not say to us what we are to do to them in regard to these.'

CHAPTER 10

[1]Then said the Most High, the Holy and Great One spake, and sent Uriel to the son of Lamech, [2]and said to him: 'Go to Noah and tell him in my name "Hide thyself!" and reveal to him the end that is approaching: that the whole earth will be destroyed, and a deluge is about to come [3]upon the whole earth, and will destroy all that is on it. And now instruct him that he may escape [4]and his seed may be preserved for all the generations of the world.' And again the Lord said to Raphael: 'Bind Azâzêl hand and foot, and cast him into the darkness: and make an opening [5]in the desert, which is in Dûdâêl, and cast him therein. And place upon him rough and jagged rocks, and cover him with darkness, and let him abide there forever, and cover his face that he may [6,7]not see light. And on the day of the great judgment he shall be cast into the fire. And heal the earth which the angels have corrupted, and proclaim the healing of the earth, that they may heal the plague, and that all the children of men may not perish through all the secret things that the [8]Watchers have disclosed and have taught their sons. And the whole earth has been corrupted [9]through the works that were taught by Azâzêl: to him ascribe all sin.' And to Gabriel said the Lord: 'Proceed against the bastards and the reprobates, and against the children of fornication: and destroy [the children of fornication and] the children of the Watchers from amongst men [and cause them to go forth]: send them one against the other that they may destroy each other in [10]battle: for length of days shall they not have. And no request that they (i.e. their fathers) make of thee shall be granted unto their fathers on their behalf; for they hope to live an eternal life, and [11]that each one of them will live five hundred years.' And the Lord said

unto Michael: 'Go, bind Semjâzâ and his associates who have united themselves with women so as to have defiled themselves [12]with them in all their uncleanness. And when their sonshave slain one another, and they have seen the destruction of their beloved ones, bind them fast for seventy generations in the valleys of the earth, till the day of their judgment and of their consummation, till the judgment that is [13]forever and ever is consummated. In those days they shall be led off to the abyss of fire: and [14]to the torment and the prison in which they shall be confined forever. And whosoever shall be condemned and destroyed will from thenceforth be bound together with them to the end of all [15]generations. And destroy all the spirits of the reprobate and the children of the Watchers, because [16]they have wronged mankind. Destroy all wrong from the face of the earth and let every evil work come to an end: and let the plant of righteousness and truth appear: and it shall prove a blessing; the works of righteousness and truth' shall be planted in truth and joy for evermore.

> [17]And then shall all the righteous escape,
> And shall live till they beget thousands of children,
> And all the days of their youth and their old age
> Shall they complete in peace.

[18]And then shall the whole earth be tilled in righteousness, and shall all be planted with trees and [19]be full of blessing. And all desirable trees shall be planted on it, and they shall plant vines on it: and the vine which they plant thereon shall yield wine in abundance, and as for all the seed which is sown thereon each measure (of it) shall bear a thousand, and each measure of olives shall yield [20]ten presses of oil. And cleanse thou the earth from all oppression, and from all unrighteousness, and from all sin, and from all godlessness: and all the uncleanness that is wrought upon the earth [21]destroy from off the earth. And all the children of men shall become righteous, and all nations [22]shall offer adoration and shall praise Me, and all shall worship Me. And the earth shall be cleansed from all defilement, and from all sin, and from all punishment, and from all torment, and I will never again send (them) upon it from generation to generation and forever.

CHAPTER 11

[1]And in those days I will open the store chambers of blessing which are in the heaven, so as to send [2]them down upon the earth over the work and labor of the children of men. And truth and peace shall be associated together throughout all the days of the world and throughout all the generations of men.'

Chapters 12-16

Dream-Vision of Enoch: his Intercession for Azâzêl and the Fallen Angels: and his Announcement of their first and final Doom

CHAPTER 12

[1]Before these things Enoch was hidden, and no one of the children of men knew where he was [2]hidden, and where he abode, and what had become of him. And his activities had to do with the Watchers, and his days were with the holy ones. [3]And I Enoch was blessing the Lord of majesty and the King of the ages, and lo! the Watchers [4]called me – Enoch the scribe– and said to me: 'Enoch, thou scribe of righteousness, go, declare to the Watchers of the heaven who have left the high heaven, the holy eternal place, and have defiled themselves with women, and have done as the children of earth do, and have taken unto themselves [5]wives: "Ye have wrought great destruction on the earth: And ye shall have no peace nor forgiveness [6]of sin: and inasmuch as they delight themselves in their children, The murder of their beloved ones shall they see, and over the destruction of their children shall they lament, and shall make supplication unto eternity, but mercy and peace shall ye not attain."

CHAPTER 13

[1]And Enoch went and said: 'Azâzêl, thou shalt have no peace: a severe sentence has gone forth [2]against thee to put thee in bonds: And thou shalt not have toleration nor request granted to thee, because of the unrighteousness which thou hast taught, and because of all the works of godlessness [3]and unrighteousness and sin which thou hast shown to men.' Then I went and spoke to them all [4]together, and they were all afraid, and fear and trembling seized them. And they besought me to draw up a petition for them that they might find forgiveness, and to read their petition in the presence [5]of the Lord of heaven. For from thenceforward they could not speak (with Him) nor lift up their [6]eyes to heaven for shame of their sins for which they had been condemned. Then I wrote out their petition, and the prayer in regard to their spirits and their deeds individually and in regard to their [7]requests that they should have forgiveness and length. And I went off and sat down at the waters of Dan, in the land of Dan, to the south of the west of Hermon: I read their petition till I fell [8]asleep. And behold a dream came to me, and visions fell down upon me, and I saw visions of chastisement, and a

voice came bidding (me) to tell it to the sons of heaven, and reprimand them. [9]And when I awaked, I came unto them, and they were all sitting gathered together, weeping in [10]Abelsjâîl, which is between Lebanon and Sênêsêr, with their faces covered. And I recounted before them all the visions which I had seen in sleep, and I began to speak the words of righteousness, and to reprimand the heavenly Watchers.

CHAPTER 14

[1]The book of the words of righteousness, and of the reprimand of the eternal Watchers in accordance [2]with the command of the Holy Great One in that vision. I saw in my sleep what I will now say with a tongue of flesh and with the breath of my mouth: which the Great One has given to men to [3]converse therewith and understand with the heart. As He has created and given to man the power of understanding the word of wisdom, so hath He created me also and given me the power of reprimanding [4]the Watchers, the children of heaven. I wrote out your petition, and in my vision it appeared thus, that your petition will not be granted unto you throughout all the days of eternity, and that judgment [5]has been finally passed upon you: yea (your petition) will not be granted unto you. And from henceforth you shall not ascend into heaven unto all eternity, and in bonds of the earth the decree [6]has gone forth to bind you for all the days of the world. And (that) previously you shall have seen the destruction of your beloved sons and ye shall have no pleasure in them, but they shall fall before [7]you by the sword. And your petition on their behalf shall not be granted, nor yet on your own: even though you weep and pray and speak all the words contained in the writing which I have [8]written. And the vision was shown to me thus: Behold, in the vision clouds invited me and a mist summoned me, and the course of the stars and the lightnings sped and hastened me, and the winds in [9]the vision caused me to fly and lifted me upward, and bore me into heaven. And I went in till I drew nigh to a wall which is built of crystals and surrounded by tongues of fire: and it began to affright [10]me. And I went into the tongues of fire and drew nigh to a large house which was built of crystals: and the walls of the house were like a tessellated floor (made) of crystals, and its groundwork was [11]of crystal. Its ceiling was like the path of the stars and the lightnings, and between them were [12]fiery cherubim, and their heaven was (clear as) water. A flaming fire surrounded the walls, and its [13]portals blazed with fire. And I entered into that house, and it was hot as fire and cold as ice: there [14]were no delights of life therein: fear covered me, and trembling gat hold upon me. And as I quaked [15]and trembled, I fell upon my face. And I beheld a vision, And lo! there was a second house, greater [16]than the former, and the entire portal stood open before me, and it was built of flames of fire. And in every respect it so excelled in splendor and

magnificence and extent that I cannot describe to [17]you its splendor and its extent. And its floor was of fire, and above it were lightnings and the path [18]of the stars, and its ceiling also was flaming fire. And I looked and saw therein a lofty throne: its appearance was as crystal, and the wheels thereof as the shining sun, and there was the vision of [19]cherubim. And from underneath the throne came streams of flaming fire so that I could not look [20]thereon. And the Great Glory sat thereon, and His raiment shone more brightly than the sun and [21]was whiter than any snow. None of the angels could enter and could behold His face by reason [22]of the magnificence and glory and no flesh could behold Him. The flaming fire was round about Him, and a great fire stood before Him, and none around could draw nigh Him: ten thousand times [23]ten thousand (stood) before Him, yet He needed no counselor. And the most holy ones who were [24]nigh to Him did not leave by night nor depart from Him. And until then I had been prostrate on my face, trembling: and the Lord called me with His own mouth, and said to me: 'Come hither, [25]Enoch, and hear my word.' And one of the holy ones came to me and waked me, and He made me rise up and approach the door: and I bowed my face downwards.

CHAPTER 15

[1]And He answered and said to me, and I heard His voice: 'Fear not, Enoch, thou righteous [2]man and scribe of righteousness: approach hither and hear my voice. And go, say to the Watchers of heaven, who have sent thee to intercede for them: "You should intercede" for men, and not men [3]for you: Wherefore have ye left the high, holy, and eternal heaven, and lain with women, and defiled yourselves with the daughters of men and taken to yourselves wives, and done like the children [4]of earth, and begotten giants (as your) sons? And though ye were holy, spiritual, living the eternal life, you have defiled yourselves with the blood of women, and have begotten (children) with the blood of flesh, and, as the children of men, have lusted after flesh and blood as those also do who die [5]and perish. Therefore have I given them wives also that they might impregnate them, and beget [6]children by them, that thus nothing might be wanting to them on earth. But you were formerly [7]spiritual, living the eternal life, and immortal for all generations of the world. And therefore I have not appointed wives for you; for as for the spiritual ones of the heaven, in heaven is their dwelling. [8]And now, the giants, who are produced from the spirits and flesh, shall be called evil spirits upon [9]the earth, and on the earth shall be their dwelling. Evil spirits have proceeded from their bodies; because they are born from men and from the holy Watchers is their beginning and primal origin; [10]they shall be evil spirits on earth, and evil spirits shall they be called. [As for the spirits of heaven, in heaven shall be their dwelling, but as for

the spirits of the earth which were born upon the earth, on the earth shall be their dwelling.] And the spirits of the giants afflict, oppress, destroy, attack, do battle, and work destruction on the earth, and cause trouble: they take no food, but nevertheless [12]hunger and thirst, and cause offences. And these spirits shall rise up against the children of men and against the women, because they have proceeded from them.

CHAPTER 16

[1]From the days of the slaughter and destruction and death of the giants, from the souls of whose flesh the spirits, having gone forth, shall destroy without incurring judgment –thus shall they destroy until the day of the consummation, the great judgment in which the age shall be [2]consummated, over the Watchers and the godless, yea, shall be wholly consummated." And now as to the watchers who have sent thee to intercede for them, who had been aforetime in heaven, (say [3]to them): "You have been in heaven, but all the mysteries had not yet been revealed to you, and you knew worthless ones, and these in the hardness of your hearts you have made known to the women, and through these mysteries women and men work much evil on earth." [4]Say to them therefore: "You have no peace."

Chapters 17-36

Enoch's Journeys through the Earth and Sheol

Chapter 17-19

The First Journey

CHAPTER 17

[1]And they took and brought me to a place in which those who were there were like flaming fire, [2]and, when they wished, they appeared as men. And they brought me to the place of darkness, and to a mountain the point of whose summit reached to heaven. And I saw the places of the luminaries and the treasuries of the stars and of the thunder and in the uttermost depths, where were [4]a fiery bow and arrows and their quiver, and a fiery sword and all the lightnings. And they took [5]me to the living waters, and to the

fire of the west, which receives every setting of the sun. And I came to a river of fire in which the fire flows like water and discharges itself into the great sea towards [6]the west. I saw the great rivers and came to the great river and to the great darkness, and went [7]to the place where no flesh walks. I saw the mountains of the darkness of winter and the place [8]whence all the waters of the deep flow. I saw the mouths of all the rivers of the earth and the mouth of the deep.

CHAPTER 18

[1]I saw the treasuries of all the winds: I saw how He had furnished with them the whole creation [2]and the firm foundations of the earth. And I saw the cornerstone of the earth: I saw the four [3]winds which bear [the earth and] the firmament of the heaven. And I saw how the winds stretch out the vaults of heaven, and have their station between heaven and earth: these are the pillars [4]of the heaven. I saw the winds of heaven which turn and bring the circumference of the sun and [5]all the stars to their setting. I saw the winds on the earth carrying the clouds: I saw the paths [6]of the angels. I saw at the end of the earth the firmament of the heaven above. And I proceeded and saw a place which burns day and night, where there are seven mountains of magnificent stones, [7]three towards the east, and three towards the south. And as for those towards the east, one was of colored stone, and one of pearl, and one of jacinth, and those towards the south of red stone. [8]But the middle one reached to heaven like the throne of God, of alabaster, and the summit of the [9,10]throne was of sapphire. And I saw a flaming fire. And beyond these mountains is a region the end of the great earth: there the heavens were completed. And I saw a deep abyss, with columns of heavenly fire, and among them I saw columns of fire fall, which were beyond measure alike towards [12]the height and towards the depth. And beyond that abyss I saw a place which had no firmament of the heaven above, and no firmly founded earth beneath it: there was no water upon it, and no [13]birds, but it was a waste and horrible place. I saw there seven stars like great burning mountains, [14]and to me, when I inquired regarding them, The angel said: 'This place is the end of heaven and [15]earth: this has become a prison for the stars and the host of heaven. And the stars which roll over the fire are they which have transgressed the commandment of the Lord in the beginning of [16]their rising, because they did not come forth at their appointed times. And He was wroth with them, and bound them till the time when their guilt should be consummated (even) for ten thousand years.'

CHAPTER 19

[1]And Uriel said to me: 'Here shall stand the angels who have connected themselves with women, and their spirits assuming many different forms are defiling mankind and shall lead them astray into sacrificing to demons as gods, (here shall they stand,) till the day of the great judgment in [2]which they shall be judged till they are made an end of. And the women also of the angels who [3]went astray shall become sirens.' And I, Enoch, alone saw the vision, the ends of all things: and no man shall see as I have seen.

CHAPTER 20

Names and Functions of the Seven Archangels

[1,2]And these are the names of the holy angels who watch. Uriel, one of the holy angels, who is [3]over the world and over Tartarus. Raphael, one of the holy angels, who is over the spirits of men. [4,5]Raguel, one of the holy angels who takes vengeance on the world of the luminaries. Michael, one [6]of the holy angels, to wit, he that is set over the best part of mankind and over chaos. Saraqâêl, [7]one of the holy angels, who is set over the spirits, who sin in the spirit. Gabriel, one of the holy [8]angels, who is over Paradise and the serpents and the Cherubim. Remiel, one of the holy angels, whom God set over those who rise.

Chapter 21-36

The Second Journey of Enoch

CHAPTER 21

Preliminary and final Place of Punishment of the fallen Angels (stars)

[1,2]And I proceeded to where things were chaotic. And I saw there something horrible: I saw neither [3]a heaven above nor a firmly founded earth, but a place chaotic and horrible. And there I saw [4]seven stars of the heaven bound together in it, like great mountains and burning with fire. Then [5]I said: 'For what sin are they bound, and on

what account have they been cast in hither?' Then said Uriel, one of the holy angels, who was with me, and was chief over them, and said: 'Enoch, why [6]dost thou ask, and why art thou eager for the truth? These are of the number of the stars of heaven, which have transgressed the commandment of the Lord, and are bound here till ten thousand years, [7]the time entailed by their sins, are consummated.' And from thence I went to another place, which was still more horrible than the former, and I saw a horrible thing: a great fire there which burnt and blazed, and the place was cleft as far as the abyss, being full of great descending columns of [8]fire: neither its extent or magnitude could I see, nor could I conjecture. Then I said: 'How [9]fearful is the place and how terrible to look upon!' Then Uriel answered me, one of the holy angels who was with me, and said unto me: 'Enoch, why hast thou such fear and affright?' And [10]I answered: 'Because of this fearful place, and because of the spectacle of the pain.' And he said unto me: 'This place is the prison of the angels, and here they will be imprisoned forever.'

CHAPTER 22

Sheol or the Underworld

[1]And thence I went to another place, and he mountain [and] of hard rock. [2]And there was in it four hollow places, deep and wide and very smooth. How smooth are the hollow places and deep and dark to look at. [3]Then Raphael answered, one of the holy angels who was with me, and said unto me: 'These hollow places have been created for this very purpose, that the spirits of the souls of the dead should [4]assemble therein, yea that all the souls of the children of men should assemble here. And these places have been made to receive them till the day of their judgment and till their appointed period [till the period appointed], till the great judgment (comes) upon them.' I saw (the spirit of) a dead man making suit, [5]and his voice went forth to heaven and made suit. And I asked Raphael the angel who was [6]with me, and I said unto him: 'This spirit which maketh suit, whose is it, whose voice goeth forth and maketh suit to heaven?' [7]And he answered me saying: 'This is the spirit which went forth from Abel, whom his brother Cain slew, and he makes his suit against him till his seed is destroyed from the face of the earth, and his seed is annihilated from amongst the seed of men.' [8]The I asked regarding it, and regarding all the hollow places: 'Why is one separated from the other?' [9]And he answered me and said unto me: 'These three have been made that the spirits of the dead might be separated. And such a division has been make (for) the spirits of the righteous, in which there is the bright spring of [10]water. And such has been made for sinners when they die and are buried in the earth and judgment has not been executed on them in their [11]lifetime. Here their spirits shall be set apart in this great pain till the

great day of judgment and punishment and torment of those who curse forever and retribution for their spirits. There [12]He shall bind them forever. And such a division has been made for the spirits of those who make their suit, who make disclosures concerning their destruction, when they were slain in the days [13]of the sinners. Such has been made for the spirits of men who were not righteous but sinners, who were complete in transgression, and of the transgressors they shall be companions: but their spirits shall not be slain in the day of judgment nor shall they be raised from thence.' [14]The I blessed the Lord of glory and said: 'Blessed be my Lord, the Lord of righteousness, who ruleth forever.'

CHAPTER 23

The fire that deals with the Luminaries of Heaven

[1,2]From thence I went to another place to the west of the ends of the earth. And I saw a burning [3]fire which ran without resting, and paused not from its course day or night but (ran) regularly. And [4]I asked saying: 'What is this which rests not?' Then Raguel, one of the holy angels who was with me, answered me and said unto me: 'This course of fire which thou hast seen is the fire in the west which persecutes all the luminaries of heaven.'

Chapter 24-25

The Seven Mountains in the North-West and the Tree of Life

CHAPTER 24

[1]And from thence I went to another place of the earth, and he showed me a mountain range of [2]fire which burnt day and night. And I went beyond it and saw seven magnificent mountains all differing each from the other, and the stones (thereof) were magnificent and beautiful, magnificent as a whole, of glorious appearance and fair exterior: three towards the east, one founded on the other, and three towards the south, one upon the other, and deep rough ravines, no one of which [3]joined with any other. And the seventh mountain was in the midst of these, and it excelled them [4]in height, resembling the seat of a throne: and fragrant trees encircled the throne. And

amongst them was a tree such as I had never yet smelt, neither was any amongst them nor were others like it: it had a fragrance beyond all fragrance, and its leaves and blooms and wood wither not for ever: [5]and its fruit is beautiful, and its fruit n resembles the dates of a palm. Then I said: 'How beautiful is this tree, and fragrant, and its leaves are fair, and its blooms very delightful in appearance.' [6]Then answered Michael, one of the holy and honored angels who was with me, and was their leader.

CHAPTER 25

[1]And he said unto me: 'Enoch, why dost thou ask me regarding the fragrance of the tree, [2]and why dost thou wish to learn the truth?' Then I answered him saying: 'I wish to [3]know about everything, but especially about this tree.' And he answered saying: 'This high mountain which thou hast seen, whose summit is like the throne of God, is His throne, where the Holy Great One, the Lord of Glory, the Eternal King, will sit, when He shall come down to visit [4]the earth with goodness. And as for this fragrant tree no mortal is permitted to touch it till the great judgment, when He shall take vengeance on all and bring (everything) to its consummation [5]forever. It shall then be given to the righteous and holy. Its fruit shall be for food to the elect: it shall be transplanted to the holy place, to the temple of the Lord, the Eternal King.

[6]Then shall they rejoice with joy and be glad,
And into the holy place shall they enter;
And its fragrance shall be in their bones,
And they shall live a long life on earth,
Such as thy fathers lived:

And in their days shall no sorrow or plague
Or torment or calamity touch them.'

[7]Then blessed I the God of Glory, the Eternal King, who hath prepared such things for the righteous, and hath created them and promised to give to them.

CHAPTER 26

Jerusalem and the Mountains, Ravines, and Streams

[1]And I went from thence to the middle of the earth, and I saw a blessed place in which there were [2]trees with branches abiding and blooming [of a dismembered tree]. And

there I saw a holy mountain, [3]and underneath the mountain to the east there was a stream and it flowed towards the south. And I saw towards the east another mountain higher than this, and between them a deep and narrow [4]ravine: in it also ran a stream underneath the mountain. And to the west thereof there was another mountain, lower than the former and of small elevation, and a ravine deep and dry between [5]them: and another deep and dry ravine was at the extremities of the three mountains. And all the ravines were deep rand narrow, (being formed) of hard rock, and trees were not planted upon [6]them. And I marveled at the rocks, and I marveled at the ravine, yea, I marveled very much.

CHAPTER 27

The Purpose of the Accursed Valley

[1]Then said I: 'For what object is this blessed land, which is entirely filled with trees, and this [2]accursed valley between?' Then Uriel, one of the holy angels who was with me, answered and said: 'This accursed valley is for those who are accursed for ever: Here shall all the accursed be gathered together who utter with their lips against the Lord unseemly words and of His glory speak hard things. Here shall they be gathered together, and here [3]shall be their place of judgment. In the last days there shall be upon them the spectacle of righteous judgment in the presence of the righteous for ever: here shall the merciful bless the Lord of glory, the Eternal King. [4]In the days of judgment over the former, they shall bless Him for the mercy in accordance with [5]which He has assigned them (their lot).' Then I blessed the Lord of Glory and set forth His glory and lauded Him gloriously.

Chapter 28-33

Further Journey to the East

CHAPTER 28

[1]And thence I went towards the east, into the midst of the mountain range of the desert, and [2]I saw a wilderness and it was solitary, full of trees and plants. And water gushed forth from [3]above. Rushing like a copious watercourse [which flowed] towards the northwest it caused clouds and dew to ascend on every side.

CHAPTER 29

[1]And thence I went to another place in the desert, and approached to the east of this mountain [2]range. And there I saw aromatic trees exhaling the fragrance of frankincense and myrrh, and the trees also were similar to the almond tree.

CHAPTER 30

[1,2]And beyond these, I went afar to the east, and I saw another place, a valley (full) of water. And [3]therein there was a tree, the color (?) of fragrant trees such as the mastic. And on the sides of those valleys I saw fragrant cinnamon. And beyond these I proceeded to the east.

CHAPTER 31

[1]And I saw other mountains, and amongst them were groves of trees, and there flowed forth from [2]them nectar, which is named sarara and galbanum. And beyond these mountains I saw another mountain to the east of the ends of the earth, whereon were aloe-trees, and all the trees were full [3]of stacte, being like almond-trees. And when one burnt it, it smelt sweeter than any fragrant odor.

CHAPTER 32

[1]And after these fragrant odors, as I looked towards the north over the mountains I saw seven mountains full of choice nard and fragrant trees and cinnamon and pepper. [2]And thence I went over the summits of all these mountains, far towards the east of the earth, and passed above the Erythraean sea and went far from it, and passed over the angel Zotiel. And I came to the Garden of Righteousness, [3]I and from afar off trees more numerous than I these trees and great-two trees there, very great, beautiful, and glorious, and magnificent, and the tree of knowledge, whose holy fruit they eat and know great wisdom. [4]That tree is in height like the fir, and its leaves are like (those of) the Carob tree: and its fruit [5]is like the clusters of the vine, very beautiful: and the fragrance of the tree penetrates afar. Then [6]I said: 'How beautiful is the tree, and how

attractive is its look!' Then Raphael the holy angel, who was with me, answered me and said: 'This is the tree of wisdom, of which thy father old (in years) and thy aged mother, who were before thee, have eaten, and they learnt wisdom and their eyes were opened, and they knew that they were naked and they were driven out of the garden.'

CHAPTER 33

[1]And from thence I went to the ends of the earth and saw there great beasts, and each differed from the other; and (I saw) birds also differing in appearance and beauty and voice, the one differing from the other. And to the east of those beasts I saw the ends of the earth whereon the heaven [2]rests, and the portals of the heaven open. And I saw how the stars of heaven come forth, and [3]I counted the portals out of which they proceed, and wrote down all their outlets, of each individual star by itself, according to their number and their names, their courses and their positions, and their [4]times and their months, as Uriel the holy angel who was with me showed me. He showed all things to me and wrote them down for me: also their names he wrote for me, and their laws and their companies.

Chapter 34-35

Enoch's Journey to the North

CHAPTER 34

[1]And from thence I went towards the north to the ends of the earth, and there I saw a great and [2]glorious device at the ends of the whole earth. And here I saw three portals of heaven open in the heaven: through each of them proceed north winds: when they blow there is cold, hail, frost, [3]snow, dew, and rain. And out of one portal they blow for good: but when they blow through the other two portals, it is with violence and affliction on the earth, and they blow with violence.

CHAPTER 35

[1]And from thence I went towards the west to the ends of the earth, and saw there three portals of the heaven open such as I had seen in the east, the same number of portals, and the same number of outlets.

CHAPTER 36

The Journey to the South

[1]And from thence I went to the south to the ends of the earth, and saw there three open portals [2]of the heaven: and thence there come dew, rain, and wind. And from thence I went to the east to the ends of the heaven, and saw here the three eastern portals of heaven open and small portals [3]above them. Through each of these small portals pass the stars of heaven and run their course to the west on the path which is shown to them. And as often as I saw I blessed always the Lord of Glory, and I continued to bless the Lord of Glory who has wrought great and glorious wonders, to show the greatness of His work to the angels and to spirits and to men, that they might praise His work and all His creation: that they might see the work of His might and praise the great work of His hands and bless Him forever.

Section 2

Chapters 37-71

The Parables

CHAPTER 37

[1]The second vision which he saw, the vision of wisdom -which Enoch the son of Jared, the son [2]of Mahalalel, the son of Cainan, the son of Enos, the son of Seth, the son of Adam, saw. And this is the beginning of the words of wisdom which I lifted up my voice to speak and say to those which dwell on earth: Hear, ye men of old time, and see, ye that come after, the words of the Holy [3]One which I will speak before the Lord of Spirits. It were better to declare (them only) to the men of old time, but even from those that come after we will not withhold the beginning of wisdom. [4]Till the present day such wisdom has never been given by the Lord of Spirits as I have received according to my insight, according to the good pleasure of the Lord of Spirits by whom the lot of [5]eternal life has been given to me. Now three Parables were imparted to me, and I lifted up my voice and recounted them to those that dwell on the earth.

Chapters 38-44

The First Parable

CHAPTER 38

The Coming Judgment of the Wicked

[1]The first Parable.

When the congregation of the righteous shall appear,
And sinners shall be judged for their sins,
And shall be driven from the face of the earth:

[2]And when the Righteous One shall appear before the eyes of the righteous,
Whose elect works hang upon the Lord of Spirits,
And light shall appear to the righteous and the elect who dwell on the earth,
Where then will be the dwelling of the sinners,
And where the resting-place of those who have denied the Lord of Spirits?
It had been good for them if they had not been born.

[3]When the secrets of the righteous shall be revealed and the sinners judged,
And the godless driven from the presence of the righteous and elect,

[4]From that time those that possess the earth shall no longer be powerful and exalted:
And they shall not be able to behold the face of the holy,
For the Lord of Spirits has caused His light to appear
On the face of the holy, righteous, and elect.

[5]Then shall the kings and the mighty perish
And be given into the hands of the righteous and holy.

[6]And thenceforward none shall seek for themselves mercy from the Lord of Spirits
For their life is at an end.

CHAPTER 39

The Abode of the Righteous and the Elect One: the Praises of
the Blessed

[1][And it shall come to pass in those days that elect and holy children will descend from the [2]high heaven, and their seed will become one with the children of men. And in those days Enoch received books of zeal and wrath, and books of disquiet and expulsion.]

And mercy shall not be accorded to them, saith the Lord of Spirits.

[3]And in those days a whirlwind carried me off from the earth,
And set me down at the end of the heavens.

[4]And there I saw another vision, the dwelling-places of the holy,
And the resting-places of the righteous.

[5]Here mine eyes saw their dwellings with His righteous angels,
And their resting-places with the holy.

And they petitioned and interceded and prayed for the children of men,
And righteousness flowed before them as water,

And mercy like dew upon the earth:
Thus it is amongst them forever and ever.

[6a]And in that place mine eyes saw the Elect One of righteousness and of faith,

[7a]And I saw his dwelling-place under the wings of the Lord of Spirits.

[6b]And righteousness shall prevail in his days,

And the righteous and elect shall be without number before Him forever and ever.

[7b]And all the righteous and elect before Him shall be strong as fiery lights,
And their mouth shall be full of blessing,

And their lips extol the name of the Lord of Spirits,
And righteousness before Him shall never fail,
[And uprightness shall never fail before Him.]

[8]There I wished to dwell,
And my spirit longed for that dwelling-place:

And there heretofore hath been my portion,
For so has it been established concerning me before the Lord of Spirits.

[9]In those days I praised and extolled the name of the Lord of Spirits with blessings and praises, because He hath destined me for blessing and glory according to the good pleasure of the Lord of [10]Spirits. For a long time my eyes regarded that place, and I blessed Him and praised Him, saying: 'Blessed is He, and may He be blessed from the beginning and for evermore. And before Him there is no ceasing. He knows before the world was created what is forever and what will be from [12]generation unto generation. Those who sleep not bless Thee: they stand before Thy glory and bless, praise, and extol, saying: "Holy, holy, holy, is the Lord of Spirits: He filleth the earth with [13]spirits."' And here my eyes saw all those who sleep not: they stand before Him and bless and say: [14]'Blessed be Thou, and blessed be the name of the Lord forever and ever.' And my face was changed; for I could no longer behold.

Chapter 40-41:2

The Four Archangels

CHAPTER 40

[1]And after that I saw thousands of thousands and ten thousand times ten thousand, I saw a multitude [2]beyond number and reckoning, who stood before the Lord of Spirits. And on the four sides of the Lord of Spirits I saw four presences, different from those that sleep not, and I learnt their names: for the angel that went with me made known to me their names, and showed me all the hidden things. [3]And I heard the voices of those four presences as they uttered praises before the Lord of glory. [4,5]The first voice blesses

the Lord of Spirits forever and ever. And the second voice I heard blessing [6]the Elect One and the elect ones who hang upon the Lord of Spirits. And the third voice I heard pray and intercede for those who dwell on the earth and supplicate in the name of the Lord of Spirits. [7]And I heard the fourth voice fending off the Satans and forbidding them to come before the Lord [8]of Spirits to accuse them who dwell on the earth. After that I asked the angel of peace who went with me, who showed me everything that is hidden: 'Who are these four presences which I have [9]seen and whose words I have heard and written down?' And he said to me: 'This first is Michael, the merciful and longsuffering: and the second, who is set over all the diseases and all the wounds of the children of men, is Raphael: and the third, who is set over all the powers, is Gabriel: and the fourth, who is set over the repentance unto hope of those who inherit eternal life, is named Phanuel.' [10]And these are the four angels of the Lord of Spirits and the four voices I heard in those days.

Chapter 41:3-9

Astronomical Secrets

CHAPTER 41

[1]And after that I saw all the secrets of the heavens, and how the kingdom is divided, and how the [2]actions of men are weighed in the balance. And there I saw the mansions of the elect and the mansions of the holy, and mine eyes saw there all the sinners being driven from thence which deny the name of the Lord of Spirits, and being dragged off: and they could not abide because of the punishment which proceeds from the Lord of Spirits. [3]And there mine eyes saw the secrets of the lightning and of the thunder, and the secrets of the winds, how they are divided to blow over the earth, and the secrets of the clouds and dew, and there [4]I saw from whence they proceed in that place and from whence they saturate the dusty earth. And there I saw closed chambers out of which the winds are divided, the chamber of the hail and winds, the chamber of the mist, and of the clouds, and the cloud thereof hovers over the earth from the [5]beginning of the world. And I saw the chambers of the sun and moon, whence they proceed and whither they come again, and their glorious return, and how one is superior to the other, and their stately orbit, and how they do not leave their orbit, and they add nothing to their orbit and they take nothing from it, and they keep faith with each other, in accordance with the oath by which they [6]are bound together. And first the sun goes forth and traverses his path according to the commandment [7]of the Lord of Spirits, and mighty is

His name forever and ever. And after that I saw the hidden and the visible path of the moon, and she accomplishes the course of her path in that place by day and by night- the one holding a position opposite to the other before the Lord of Spirits.

And they give thanks and praise and rest not;
For unto them is their thanksgiving rest.

[8]For the sun changes oft for a blessing or a curse,
And the course of the path of the moon is light to the righteous
And darkness to the sinners in the name of the Lord,
Who made a separation between the light and the darkness,
And divided the spirits of men,
And strengthened the spirits of the righteous,
In the name of His righteousness.

[9]For no angel hinders and no power is able to hinder; for He appoints a judge for them all and He judges them all before Him.

CHAPTER 42

The Dwelling-places of Wisdom and of Unrighteousness

[1]Wisdom found no place where she might dwell;
Then a dwelling-place was assigned her in the heavens.

[2]Wisdom went forth to make her dwelling among the children of men,
And found no dwelling-place:

Wisdom returned to her place,
And took her seat among the angels.

[3]And unrighteousness went forth from her chambers:
Whom she sought not she found,
And dwelt with them,

As rain in a desert
And dew on a thirsty land.

Chapter 43-44

Astronomical Secrets

CHAPTER 43

[1]And I saw other lightnings and the stars of heaven, and I saw how He called them all by their [2]names and they hearkened unto Him. And I saw how they are weighed in a righteous balance according to their proportions of light: (I saw) the width of their spaces and the day of their appearing, and how their revolution produces lightning: and (I saw) their revolution according to the [3]number of the angels, and (how) they keep faith with each other. And I asked the angel who went [4]with me who showed me what was hidden: 'What are these?' And he said to me: 'The Lord of Spirits hath showed thee their parabolic meaning (lit. 'their parable'): these are the names of the holy who dwell on the earth and believe in the name of the Lord of Spirits forever and ever.'

CHAPTER 44

[1]Also another phenomenon I saw in regard to the lightnings: how some of the stars arise and become lightnings and cannot part with their new form.

Chapters 45-57

The Second Parable

CHAPTER 45

*The Lot of the Apostates: the New Heaven
and the New Earth*

[1]And this is the second Parable concerning those who deny the name of the dwelling of the holy ones and the Lord of Spirits.

[2]And into the heaven they shall not ascend,
And on the earth they shall not come:
Such shall be the lot of the sinners
Who have denied the name of the Lord of Spirits,
Who are thus preserved for the day of suffering and tribulation.

[3]On that day Mine Elect One shall sit on the throne of glory

And shall try their works,
And their places of rest shall be innumerable.

And their souls shall grow strong within them when they see Mine Elect Ones,
And those who have called upon My glorious name:

⁴Then will I cause Mine Elect One to dwell among them.
And I will transform the heaven and make it an eternal blessing and light

⁵And I will transform the earth and make it a blessing:

And I will cause Mine elect ones to dwell upon it:
But the sinners and evildoers shall not set foot thereon.

⁶For I have provided and satisfied with peace My righteous ones
And have caused them to dwell before Me:

But for the sinners there is judgment impending with Me,
So that I shall destroy them from the face of the earth.

CHAPTER 46

The Head of Days and the Son of Man

¹And there I saw One who had a head of days,
And His head was white like wool,
And with Him was another being whose countenance had the appearance of a man,
And his face was full of graciousness, like one of the holy angels.

²And I asked the angel who went with me and showed me all the hidden things, concerning that

³Son of Man, who he was, and whence he was, (and) why he went with the Head of Days? And he answered and said unto me:

This is the son of Man who hath righteousness,

With whom dwelleth righteousness,
And who revealeth all the treasures of that which is hidden,

Because the Lord of Spirits hath chosen him,

And whose lot hath the preeminence before the Lord of Spirits in uprightness forever.

[4]And this Son of Man whom thou hast seen
Shall raise up the kings and the mighty from their seats,
[And the strong from their thrones]
And shall loosen the reins of the strong,
And break the teeth of the sinners.

[5][And he shall put down the kings from their thrones and kingdoms]
Because they do not extol and praise Him,
Nor humbly acknowledge whence the kingdom was bestowed upon them.

[6]And he shall put down the countenance of the strong,
And shall fill them with shame.

And darkness shall be their dwelling,
And worms shall be their bed,
And they shall have no hope of rising from their beds,
Because they do not extol the name of the Lord of Spirits.

[7]And these are they who judge the stars of heaven,
[And raise their hands against the Most High],
And tread upon the earth and dwell upon it.
And all their deeds manifest unrighteousness,
And their power rests upon their riches,
And their faith is in the gods which they have made with their hands,
And they deny the name of the Lord of Spirits,

[8]And they persecute the houses of His congregations,
And the faithful who hang upon the name of the Lord of Spirits.

CHAPTER 47

The Prayer of the Righteous for Vengeance and their Joy at its coming

[1]And in those days shall have ascended the prayer of the righteous,
And the blood of the righteous from the earth before the Lord of Spirits.

[2]In those days the holy ones who dwell above in the heavens
Shall unite with one voice
And supplicate and pray [and praise,
And give thanks and bless the name of the Lord of Spirits
On behalf of the blood of the righteous which has been shed,

And that the prayer of the righteous may not be in vain before the Lord of Spirits,
That judgment may be done unto them,
And that they may not have to suffer forever.

³In those days I saw the Head of Days when He seated himself upon the throne of His glory,
And the books of the living were opened before Him:
And all His host which is in heaven above and His counselors stood before Him,

⁴And the hearts of the holy were filled with joy;
Because the number of the righteous had been offered,
And the prayer of the righteous had been heard,
And the blood of the righteous been required before the Lord of Spirits.

CHAPTER 48

The Fount of Righteousness: the Son of Man -the Stay of the Righteous: Judgment of the Kings and the Mighty

¹And in that place I saw the fountain of righteousness
Which was inexhaustible:
And around it were many fountains of wisdom:
And all the thirsty drank of them,
And were filled with wisdom,
And their dwellings were with the righteous and holy and elect.

²And at that hour that Son of Man was named
In the presence of the Lord of Spirits,
And his name before the Head of Days.

³Yea, before the sun and the signs were created,
Before the stars of the heaven were made,
His name was named before the Lord of Spirits.

⁴He shall be a staff to the righteous whereon to stay themselves and not fall,
And he shall be the light of the Gentiles,
And the hope of those who are troubled of heart.

⁵All who dwell on earth shall fall down and worship before him,
And will praise and bless and celebrate with song the Lord of Spirits.

[6]And for this reason hath he been chosen and hidden before Him,
Before the creation of the world and for evermore.

[7]And the wisdom of the Lord of Spirits hath revealed him to the holy and righteous;
For he hath preserved the lot of the righteous,
Because they have hated and despised this world of unrighteousness,
And have hated all its works and ways in the name of the Lord of Spirits:
For in his name they are saved,
And according to his good pleasure hath it been in regard to their life.

[8]In these days downcast in countenance shall the kings of the earth have become,
And the strong who possess the land because of the works of their hands,
For on the day of their anguish and affliction they shall not (be able to) save themselves.

[9]And I will give them over into the hands of Mine elect:
As straw in the fire so shall they burn before the face of the holy:
As lead in the water shall they sink before the face of the righteous,
And no trace of them shall any more be found.

[10]And on the day of their affliction there shall be rest on the earth,
And before them they shall fall and not rise again:
And there shall be no one to take them with his hands and raise them:
For they have denied the Lord of Spirits and His Anointed.
The name of the Lord of Spirits be blessed.

CHAPTER 49

The Power and Wisdom of the Elect One

[1]For wisdom is poured out like water,
And glory faileth not before him for evermore.

[2]For he is mighty in all the secrets of righteousness,
And unrighteousness shall disappear as a shadow,
And have no continuance;
Because the Elect One standeth before the Lord of Spirits,
And his glory is forever and ever,
And his might unto all generations.

³And in him dwells the spirit of wisdom,
And the spirit which gives insight,
And the spirit of understanding and of might,
And the spirit of those who have fallen asleep in righteousness.

⁴And he shall judge the secret things,
And none shall be able to utter a lying word before him;
For he is the Elect One before the Lord of Spirits according to His good pleasure.

CHAPTER 50

*The Glorification and Victory of the Righteous: the
Repentance of the Gentiles*

¹And in those days a change shall take place for the holy and elect,
And the light of days shall abide upon them,
And glory and honor shall turn to the holy,

²On the day of affliction on which evil shall have been treasured up against the sinners.

And the righteous shall be victorious in the name of the Lord of Spirits:
And He will cause the others to witness (this)
That they may repent
And forgo the works of their hands.

³They shall have no honor through the name of the Lord of Spirits,
Yet through His name shall they be saved,
And the Lord of Spirits will have compassion on them,
For His compassion is great.

⁴And He is righteous also in His judgment,
And in the presence of His glory unrighteousness also shall not maintain itself:
At His judgment the unrepentant shall perish before Him.

⁵And from henceforth I will have no mercy on them, saith the Lord of Spirits.

CHAPTER 51

*The Resurrection of the Dead, and the Separation by the
Judge of the Righteous and the Wicked*

[1]And in those days shall the earth also give back that which has been entrusted to it,

And Sheol also shall give back that which it has received,
And hell shall give back that which it owes.

[5a]For in those days the Elect One shall arise,

[2]And he shall choose the righteous and holy from among them:
For the day has drawn nigh that they should be saved.

[3]And the Elect One shall in those days sit on My throne,
And his mouth shall pour forth all the secrets of wisdom and counsel:
For the Lord of Spirits hath given (them) to him and hath glorified him.

[4]And in those days shall the mountains leap like rams,
And the hills also shall skip like lambs satisfied with milk,
And the faces of [all] the angels in heaven shall be lighted up with joy.

[5b]And the earth shall rejoice,

[c]And the righteous shall dwell upon it,

[d]And the elect shall walk thereon.

CHAPTER 52

The Seven Metal Mountains and the Elect One

[1]And after those days in that place where I had seen all the visions of that which is hidden -for [2]I had been carried off in a whirlwind and they had borne me towards the west -There mine eyes saw all the secret things of heaven that shall be, a mountain of iron, and a mountain of copper, and a mountain of silver, and a mountain of gold, and a mountain of soft metal, and a mountain of lead. [3]And I asked the angel who went with me, saying, 'What things are these which I have seen in [4]secret?' And he said unto me: 'All these things which thou hast seen shall serve the dominion of His Anointed that he may be potent and mighty on the earth.' [5]And that angel of peace answered, saying

unto me: 'Wait a little, and there shall be revealed unto thee all the secret things which surround the Lord of Spirits.

[6]And these mountains which thine eyes have seen,
The mountain of iron, and the mountain of copper, and the mountain of silver,
And the mountain of gold, and the mountain of soft metal, and the mountain of lead,
All these shall be in the presence of the Elect One
As wax: before the fire,
And like the water which streams down from above [upon those mountains],
And they shall become powerless before his feet.

[7]And it shall come to pass in those days that none shall be saved,
Either by gold or by silver,
And none be able to escape.

[8]And there shall be no iron for war,
Nor shall one clothe oneself with a breastplate.
Bronze shall be of no service,
And tin [shall be of no service and] shall not be esteemed,
And lead shall not be desired.

[9]And all these things shall be [denied and] destroyed from the surface of the earth,
When the Elect One shall appear before the face of the Lord of Spirits.'

Chapter 53-54

The Valley of Judgment: the Angels of Punishment: the Communities of the Elect One

CHAPTER 53

[1]There mine eyes saw a deep valley with open mouths, and all who dwell on the earth and sea and islands shall bring to him gifts and presents and tokens of homage, but that deep valley shall not become full.

[2]And their hands commit lawless deeds,
And the sinners devour all whom they lawlessly oppress:
Yet the sinners shall be destroyed before the face of the Lord of Spirits,

And they shall be banished from off the face of His earth,
And they shall perish forever and ever.

[3]For I saw all the angels of punishment abiding (there) and preparing all the instruments of Satan. [4]And I asked the angel of peace who went with me: 'For whom are they preparing these Instruments?' [5]And he said unto me: 'They prepare these for the kings and the mighty of this earth, that they may thereby be destroyed. [6]And after this the Righteous and Elect One shall cause the house of his congregation to appear: henceforth they shall be no more hindered in the name of the Lord of Spirits.

[7]And these mountains shall not stand as the earth before his righteousness,
But the hills shall be as a fountain of water,
And the righteous shall have rest from the oppression of sinners.'

CHAPTER 54

[1]And I looked and turned to another part of the earth, and saw there a deep valley with burning [2]fire. And they brought the kings and the mighty, and began to cast them into this deep valley. [3]And there mine eyes saw how they made these their instruments, iron chains of immeasurable weight. [4]And I asked the angel of peace who went with me, saying: 'For whom are these chains being prepared?' And he said unto me: 'These are being prepared for the hosts of Azâzêl, so that they may take them and cast them into the abyss of complete condemnation, and they shall cover their jaws with rough stones as the Lord of Spirits commanded. [6]And Michael, and Gabriel, and Raphael, and Phanuel shall take hold of them on that great day, and cast them on that day into the burning furnace, that the Lord of Spirits may take vengeance on them for their unrighteousness in becoming subject to Satan and leading astray those who dwell on the earth.'

Chapter 54:7-55:2

Noachic Fragment on the first World Judgment

[7]And in those days shall punishment come from the Lord of Spirits, and he will open all the chambers of waters which are above the heavens, and of the fountains which are beneath the earth. [8]And all the waters shall be joined with the waters: that which is above the heavens is the masculine, [9]and the water which is beneath the earth is the feminine. And they shall destroy all who dwell [10]on the earth and those who dwell

under the ends of the heaven. And when they have recognized their unrighteousness which they have wrought on the earth, then by these shall they perish.

Chapter 55:3-56:4

Final Judgment of Azazel, the Watchers and their children

CHAPTER 55

[1]And after that the Head of Days repented and said: 'In vain have I destroyed all who dwell [2]on the earth.' And He sware by His great name: 'Henceforth I will not do so to all who dwell on the earth, and I will set a sign in the heaven: and this shall be a pledge of good faith between Me and them forever, so long as heaven is above the earth. And this is in accordance with My command. [3]When I have desired to take hold of them by the hand of the angels on the day of tribulation and pain because of this, I will cause My chastisement and My wrath to abide upon them, saith [4]God, the Lord of Spirits. Ye mighty kings who dwell on the earth, ye shall have to behold Mine Elect One, how he sits on the throne of glory and judges Azâzêl, and all his associates, and all his hosts in the name of the Lord of Spirits.'

CHAPTER 56

[1]And I saw there the hosts of the angels of punishment going, and they held scourges and chains [2]of iron and bronze. And I asked the angel of peace who went with me, saying: 'To whom are [3]these who hold the scourges going?' And he said unto me: 'To their elect and beloved ones, that they may be cast into the chasm of the abyss of the valley.

[4]And then that valley shall be filled with their elect and beloved,
And the days of their lives shall be at an end,
And the days of their leading astray shall not thenceforward be reckoned.

Chapter 56:5-8

Last Struggle of the Heathen Powers against Israel

[5]And in those days the angels shall return
And hurl themselves to the east upon the Parthians and Medes:

They shall stir up the kings, so that a spirit of unrest shall come upon them,
And they shall rouse them from their thrones,

That they may break forth as lions from their lairs,
And as hungry wolves among their flocks.

[6]And they shall go up and tread underfoot the land of His elect ones [And the land of His elect ones shall be before them a threshing-floor and a highway:]

[7]But the city of my righteous shall be a hindrance to their horses.

And they shall begin to fight among themselves,
And their right hand shall be strong against themselves,

And a man shall not know his brother,
Nor a son his father or his mother,

Till there be no number of the corpses through their slaughter,
And their punishment be not in vain.

[8]In those days Sheol shall open its jaws,
And they shall be swallowed up therein

And their destruction shall be at an end;
Sheol shall devour the sinners in the presence of the elect.'

CHAPTER 57

The Return from the Dispersion

[1]And it came to pass after this that I saw another host of wagons, and men riding thereon, and [2]coming on the winds from the east, and from the west to the south. And the noise of their wagons was heard, and when this turmoil took place the holy ones from heaven remarked it, and the pillars of the earth were moved from their place, and the sound thereof was heard from the one end of heaven [3]to the other, in one day. And they shall all fall down and worship the Lord of Spirits. And this is the end of the second Parable.

Chapters 58-71

The Third Parable

CHAPTER 58

The Blessedness of the Saints

¹And I began to speak the third Parable concerning the righteous and elect.

²Blessed are ye, ye righteous and elect,
For glorious shall be your lot.

³And the righteous shall be in the light of the sun.
And the elect in the light of eternal life:
The days of their life shall be unending,
And the days of the holy without number.

⁴And they shall seek the light and find righteousness with the Lord of Spirits:
There shall be peace to the righteous in the name of the Eternal Lord.

⁵And after this it shall be said to the holy in heaven
That they should seek out the secrets of righteousness, the heritage of faith:
For it has become bright as the sun upon earth,
And the darkness is past.

⁶And there shall be a light that never endeth,
And to a limit (lit. 'number') of days they shall not come,
For the darkness shall first have been destroyed,
[And the light established before the Lord of Spirits]
And the light of uprightness established for ever before the Lord of Spirits.

CHAPTER 59

The Lights and the Thunder

¹[In those days mine eyes saw the secrets of the lightnings, and of the lights, and the judgments they execute (lit. 'their judgment'): and they lighten for a blessing or a curse as the Lord of ²Spirits willeth. And there I saw the secrets of the thunder, and how when it resounds above in the heaven, the sound thereof is heard, and he caused me to

see the judgments executed on the earth, whether they be for wellbeing and blessing, or for a curse according to the word of the Lord of Spirits. [3]And after that all the secrets of the lights and lightnings were shown to me, and they lighten for blessing and for satisfying.]

Book of Noah -a Fragment

CHAPTER 60

Quaking of the Heaven: Behemoth and
Leviathan: the Elements.

[1]In the year 500, in the seventh month, on the fourteenth day of the month in the life of Enoch. In that Parable I saw how a mighty quaking made the heaven of heavens to quake, and the host of the Most High, and the angels, a thousand thousands and ten thousand times ten thousand, were [2]disquieted with a great disquiet. And the Head of Days sat on the throne of His glory, and the angels and the righteous stood around Him.

[3]And a great trembling seized me,
And fear took hold of me,
And my loins gave way,
And dissolved were my reins,
And I fell upon my face.

[4]And Michael sent another angel from among the holy ones and he raised me up, and when he had raised me up my spirit returned; for I had not been able to endure the look of this host, and the [5]commotion and the quaking of the heaven. And Michael said unto me: 'Why art thou disquieted with such a vision? Until this day lasted the day of His mercy; and He hath been merciful and [6]longsuffering towards those who dwell on the earth. And when the day, and the power, and the punishment, and the judgment come, which the Lord of Spirits hath prepared for those who worship not the righteous law, and for those who deny the righteous judgment, and for those who take His name in vain-that day is prepared, for the elect a covenant, but for sinners an inquisition. [25]When the punishment of the Lord of Spirits shall rest upon them, it shall rest in order that the punishment of the Lord of Spirits may not come, in vain, and it shall slay the children with their mothers and the children with their fathers. Afterwards the judgment shall take place according to His mercy and His patience.' [7]And on that day

were two monsters parted, a female monster named Leviathan, to dwell in the [8]abysses of the ocean over the fountains of the waters. But the male is named Behemoth, who occupied with his breast a waste wilderness named Duidain, on the east of the garden where the elect and righteous dwell, where my grandfather was taken up, the seventh from Adam, the first [9]man whom the Lord of Spirits created. And I besought the other angel that he should show me the might of those monsters, how they were parted on one day and cast, the one into the abysses [10]of the sea, and the other unto the dry land of the wilderness. And he said to me: 'Thou son of man, herein thou dost seek to know what is hidden.' [11]And the other angel who went with me and showed me what was hidden told me what is first and last in the heaven in the height, and beneath the earth in the depth, and at the ends of the [12]heaven, and on the foundation of the heaven. And the chambers of the winds, and how the winds are divided, and how they are weighed, and (how) the portals of the winds are reckoned, each according to the power of the wind, and the power of the lights of the moon, and according to the power that is fitting: and the divisions of the stars according to their names, and how all the divisions [13]are divided. And the thunders according to the places where they fall, and all the divisions that are made among the lightnings that it may lighten, and their host that they may at once obey. [14]For the thunder has places of rest (which) are assigned (to it) while it is waiting for its peal; and the thunder and lightning are inseparable, and although not one and undivided, they both go together [15]through the spirit and separate not. For when the lightning lightens, the thunder utters its voice, and the spirit enforces a pause during the peal, and divides equally between them; for the treasury of their peals is like the sand, and each one of them as it peals is held in with a bridle, and turned back by the power of the spirit, and pushed forward according to the many quarters of the earth. [16]And the spirit of the sea is masculine and strong, and according to the might of his strength he draws it back with a rein, and in like manner it is driven forward and disperses amid all the mountains [17]of the earth. And the spirit of the hoarfrost is his own angel, and the spirit of the hail is a good [18]angel. And the spirit of the snow has forsaken his chambers on account of his strength -There is a [19]special spirit therein, and that which ascends from it is like smoke, and its name is frost. And the spirit of the mist is not united with them in their chambers, but it has a special chamber; for its course is glorious both in light and in darkness, and in winter and in summer, and in its chamber is an angel. [20]And the spirit of the dew has its dwelling at the ends of the heaven, and is connected with the chambers of the rain, and its course is in winter and summer: and its clouds and the clouds of the [21]mist are connected, and the one gives to the other. And when the spirit of the rain goes forth from its chamber, the angels come and open the chamber and lead it out, and when it is diffused over the whole earth it unites with the water on the earth. And whensoever it unites with the water on [22]the earth... For the waters are for those who dwell on the earth; for they are nourishment for the earth from the Most High who is in heaven: therefore there is a measure for the rain, [23]and the angels take it in charge. And these things I saw towards the Garden of the Righteous. [24]And the angel of peace who was with me said to me: 'These two monsters, prepared conformably to the greatness of God, shall feed...

CHAPTER 61

Angels go off to measure Paradise: the Judgment of the Righteous by the
Elect One: the Praise of the Elect One and of God

[1]And I saw in those days how long cords were given to those angels, and they took to themselves wings and flew, and they went towards the north. [2]And I asked the angel, saying unto him: 'Why have those (angels) taken these cords and gone off?' And he said unto me: 'They have gone to measure.'

[3]And the angel who went with me said unto me:
'These shall bring the measures of the righteous,
And the ropes of the righteous to the righteous,
That they may stay themselves on the name of the Lord of Spirits forever and ever.

[4]The elect shall begin to dwell with the elect,
And those are the measures which shall be given to faith
And which shall strengthen righteousness.

[5]And these measures shall reveal all the secrets of the depths of the earth,
And those who have been destroyed by the desert,
And those who have been devoured by the beasts,
And those who have been devoured by the fish of the sea,
That they may return and stay themselves
On the day of the Elect One;
For none shall be destroyed before the Lord of Spirits,
And none can be destroyed.

[6]And all who dwell above in the heaven received a command and power and one voice and one light like unto fire.

[7]And that One (with) their first words they blessed,
And extolled and lauded with wisdom,
And they were wise in utterance and in the spirit of life.

[8]And the Lord of Spirits placed the Elect one on the throne of glory.
And he shall judge all the works of the holy above in the heaven,

And in the balance shall their deeds be weighed

⁹And when he shall lift up his countenance
To judge their secret ways according to the word of the name of the Lord of Spirits,
And their path according to the way of the righteous judgment of the Lord of Spirits,
Then shall they all with one voice speak and bless,
And glorify and extol and sanctify the name of the Lord of Spirits.

¹⁰And He will summon all the host of the heavens, and all the holy ones above, and the host of God, the Cherubic, Seraphin and Ophannin, and all the angels of power, and all the angels of principalities, ¹¹and the Elect One, and the other powers on the earth (and) over the water. On that day shall raise one voice, and bless and glorify and exalt in the spirit of faith, and in the spirit of wisdom, and in the spirit of patience, and in the spirit of mercy, and in the spirit of judgment and of peace, and in the spirit of goodness, and shall all say with one voice: "Blessed is He, and may the name of the Lord of Spirits be blessed forever and ever."

¹²All who sleep not above in heaven shall bless Him:
All the holy ones who are in heaven shall bless Him,
And all the elect who dwell in the garden of life:

And every spirit of light who is able to bless, and glorify, and extol, and hallow Thy blessed name,
And all flesh shall beyond measure glorify and bless Thy name forever and ever.

¹³For great is the mercy of the Lord of Spirits, and He is longsuffering,
And all His works and all that He has created He has revealed to the righteous and elect
In the name of the Lord of Spirits.'

CHAPTER 62

Judgment of the Kings and the Mighty:
Blessedness of the Righteous

¹And thus the Lord commanded the kings and the mighty and the exalted, and those who dwell on the earth, and said:

'Open your eyes and lift up your horns if ye are able to recognize the Elect One.'

[2]And the Lord of Spirits seated him on the throne of His glory,
And the spirit of righteousness was poured out upon him,
And the word of his mouth slays all the sinners,
And all the unrighteous are destroyed from before his face.

[3]And there shall stand up in that day all the kings and the mighty,
And the exalted and those who hold the earth,
And they shall see and recognize How he sits on the throne of his glory,
And righteousness is judged before him,
And no lying word is spoken before him.

[4]Then shall pain come upon them as on a woman in travail,
[And she has pain in bringing forth]
When her child enters the mouth of the womb,
And she has pain in bringing forth.

[5]And one portion of them shall look on the other,
And they shall be terrified,
And they shall be downcast of countenance,
And pain shall seize them,
When they see that Son of Man Sitting on the throne of his glory.

[6]And the kings and the mighty and all who possess the earth shall bless and glorify and extol him who rules over all, who was hidden.

[7]For from the beginning the Son of Man was hidden,
And the Most High preserved him in the presence of His might,
And revealed him to the elect.

[8]And the congregation of the elect and holy shall be sown,
And all the elect shall stand before him on that day.

[9]And all the kings and the mighty and the exalted and those who rule the earth
Shall fall down before him on their faces,
And worship and set their hope upon that Son of Man,
And petition him and supplicate for mercy at his hands.

[10]Nevertheless that Lord of Spirits will so press them
That they shall hastily go forth from His presence,
And their faces shall be filled with shame,
And the darkness grow deeper on their faces.

[11]And He will deliver them to the angels for punishment,
To execute vengeance on them because they have oppressed His children and His elect

¹²And they shall be a spectacle for the righteous and for His elect:
They shall rejoice over them,
Because the wrath of the Lord of Spirits resteth upon them,
And His sword is drunk with their blood.

¹³And the righteous and elect shall be saved on that day,
And they shall never thenceforward see the face of the sinners and unrighteous.

¹⁴And the Lord of Spirits will abide over them,
And with that Son of Man shall they eat
And lie down and rise up forever and ever.

¹⁵And the righteous and elect shall have risen from the earth,
And ceased to be of downcast countenance.

And they shall have been clothed with garments of glory,

¹⁶And these shall be the garments of life from the Lord of Spirits:
And your garments shall not grow old,
Nor your glory pass away before the Lord of Spirits.

CHAPTER 63

The unavailing Repentance of the Kingsand the Mighty

¹In those days shall the mighty and the kings who possess the earth implore (Him) to grant them a little respite from His angels of punishment to whom they were delivered, that they might fall

²down and worship before the Lord of Spirits, and confess their sins before Him. And they shall bless and glorify the Lord of Spirits, and say:

' Blessed is the Lord of Spirits and the Lord of kings,
And the Lord of the mighty and the Lord of the rich,
And the Lord of glory and the Lord of wisdom,

³And splendid in every secret thing is Thy power from generation to generation,
And Thy glory forever and ever:

Deep are all Thy secrets and innumerable,
And Thy righteousness is beyond reckoning.

⁴We have now learnt that we should glorify
And bless the Lord of kings and Him who is king over all kings.'

[5]And they shall say:
'Would that we had rest to glorify and give thanks
And confess our faith before His glory!

[6]And now we long for a little rest but find it not:
We follow hard upon and obtain (it) not:

And light has vanished from before us,
And darkness is our dwelling-place forever and ever:

[7]For we have not believed before Him
Nor glorified the name of the Lord of Spirits, [nor glorified our Lord]

But our hope was in the scepter of our kingdom,
And in our glory.

[8]And in the day of our suffering and tribulation He saves us not,
And we find no respite for confession

That our Lord is true in all His works, and in His judgments and His justice,
And His judgments have no respect of persons.

[9]And we pass away from before His face on account of our works,
And all our sins are reckoned up in righteousness.'

[10]Now they shall say unto themselves: 'Our souls are full of unrighteous gain, but it does not prevent us from descending from the midst thereof into the burden of Sheol.'

[11]And after that their faces shall be filled with darkness
And shame before that Son of Man,
And they shall be driven from his presence,
And the sword shall abide before his face in their midst.

[12]Thus spake the Lord of Spirits: 'This is the ordinance and judgment with respect to the mighty and the kings and the exalted and those who possess the earth before the Lord of Spirits.'

CHAPTER 64

Vision of the Fallen Angels in the Place of Punishment

[1,2]And other forms I saw hidden in that place. I heard the voice of the angel saying: 'These are the angels who descended to the earth, and revealed what was hidden to the children of men and seduced the children of men into committing sin.'

CHAPTER 65

Enoch foretells to Noah the Deluge and his own Preservation

[1,2]And in those days Noah saw the earth that it had sunk down and its destruction was nigh. And he arose from thence and went to the ends of the earth, and cried aloud to his grandfather Enoch: [3]and Noah said three times with an embittered voice: 'Hear me, hear me, hear me.' And I said unto him: 'Tell me what it is that is falling out on the earth that the earth is in such evil plight [4]and shaken, lest perchance I shall perish with it?' And thereupon there was a great commotion, on the earth, and a voice was heard from heaven, and I fell on my face. And Enoch my grandfather came and stood by me, and said unto me: 'Why hast thou cried unto me with a bitter cry and weeping [6]And a command has gone forth from the presence of the Lord concerning those who dwell on the earth that their ruin is accomplished because they have learnt all the secrets of the angels, and all the violence of the Satans, and all their powers -the most secret ones- and all the power of those who practice sorcery, and the power of witchcraft, and the power of those who make molten images [7]for the whole earth: And how silver is produced from the dust of the earth, and how soft metal [8]originates in the earth. For lead and tin are not produced from the earth like the first: it is a fountain [9]that produces them, and an angel stands therein, and that angel is preeminent.' And after that my grandfather Enoch took hold of me by my hand and raised me up, and said unto me: 'Go, for I have [10]asked the Lord of Spirits as touching this commotion on the earth. And He said unto me: "Because of their unrighteousness their judgment has been determined upon and shall not be withheld by Me forever. Because of the sorceries which they have searched out and learnt, the earth and those [11]who dwell upon it shall be destroyed." And these -they have no place of repentance forever, because they have shown them what was hidden, and they are the damned: but as for thee, my son, the Lord of Spirits knows that thou art pure, and guiltless of this reproach concerning the secrets.

[12]And He has destined thy name to be among the holy,
And will preserve thee amongst those who dwell on the earth,
And has destined thy righteous seed both for kingship and for great honors,
And from thy seed shall proceed a fountain of the righteous and holy without number forever.

CHAPTER 66

The Angels of the Waters bidden to hold them in Check

[1]And after that he showed me the angels of punishment who are prepared to come and let loose all the powers of the waters which are beneath in the earth in order to bring judgment and destruction [2]on all who [abide and] dwell on the earth. And the Lord of Spirits gave commandment to the angels who were going forth, that they should not cause the waters to rise but should hold them [3]in check; for those angels were over the powers of the waters. And I went away from the presence of Enoch.

CHAPTER 67

God's Promise to Noah: Places of Punishment of the Angels
and of the Kings

[1]And in those days the word of God came unto me, and He said unto me: 'Noah, thy lot has come [2]up before Me, a lot without blame, a lot of love and uprightness. And now the angels are making a wooden (building), and when they have completed that task I will place My hand upon it and preserve it, and there shall come forth from it the seed of life, and a change shall set in so that the [3]earth will not remain without inhabitant. And I will make fast thy sed before me forever and ever, and I will spread abroad those who dwell with thee: it shall not be unfruitful on the face of the earth, but it shall be blessed and multiply on the earth in the name of the Lord.' [4]And He will imprison those angels, who have shown unrighteousness, in that burning valley which my grandfather Enoch had formerly shown to me in the west among the mountains of gold [5]and silver and iron and soft metal and tin. And I saw that valley in which there was a great [6]convulsion and a convulsion of the waters. And when all this took place, from that fiery molten metal and from the convulsion thereof in that place, there was produced a smell of sulfur, and it was connected with those waters, and that valley of the angels who had led astray (mankind) burned [7]beneath that land. And through its valleys proceed streams of fire, where these angels are punished who had led astray those who dwell upon the earth. [8]But those waters shall in those days serve for the kings and the mighty and the exalted, and those who dwell on the earth, for the healing of the body, but for the punishment of the spirit; now their spirit is full of lust, that they may be punished in their body, for they have denied the Lord of Spirits [9]and see their punishment daily, and yet believe not in His name. And in proportion as the burning of their bodies becomes severe, a corresponding change shall take place in their

spirit forever and ever; [10]for before the Lord of Spirits none shall utter an idle word. For the judgment shall come upon them, [11]because they believe in the lust of their body and deny the Spirit of the Lord. And those same waters will undergo a change in those days; for when those angels are punished in these waters, these water-springs shall change their temperature, and when the angels ascend, this water of the [12]springs shall change and become cold. And I heard Michael answering and saying: ' This judgment wherewith the angels are judged is a testimony for the kings and the mighty who possess the [13]earth.' Because these waters of judgment minister to the healing of the body of the kings and the lust of their body; therefore they will not see and will not believe that those waters will change and become a fire which burns forever.

CHAPTER 68

Michael and Raphael astonished at the Severity of the Judgment

[1]And after that my grandfather Enoch gave me the teaching of all the secrets in the book in the Parables which had been given to him, and he put them together for me in the words of the book [2]of the Parables. And on that day Michael answered Raphael and said: 'The power of the spirit transports and makes me to tremble because of the severity of the judgment of the secrets, the judgment of the angels: who can endure the severe judgment which has been executed, and before [3]which they melt away?' And Michael answered again, and said to Raphael: 'Who is he whose heart is not softened concerning it, and whose reins are not troubled by this word of judgment [4](that) has gone forth upon them because of those who have thus led them out?' And it came to pass when he stood before the Lord of Spirits, Michael said thus to Raphael: 'I will not take their part under the eye of the Lord; for the Lord of Spirits has been angry with them because they do [5]as if they were the Lord. Therefore all that is hidden shall come upon them forever and ever; for neither angel nor man shall have his portion (in it), but alone they have received their judgment forever and ever.

CHAPTER 69

*The Names and Functions of the (fallen Angels and) Satans:
the secret Oath*

[1]And after this judgment they shall terrify and make them to tremble because they have shown this to those who dwell on the earth. [2]And behold the names of those angels

[and these are their names: the first of them is Samjâzâ, the second Artâqîfâ, and the third Armen, the fourth Kôkabêl, the fifth Tûrâêl, the sixth Rûmjâl, the seventh Dânjâl, the eighth Nêqâêl, the ninth Barâqêl, the tenth Azâzêl, the eleventh Armârôs, the twelfth Batarjâl, the thirteenth Busasêjal, the fourteenth Hanânêl, the fifteenth Tûrêl, and the sixteenth Sîmâpêsîêl, the seventeenth Jetrêl, the eighteenth Tûmêêl, the nineteenth Tûrêl, [3]the twentieth Rûmâêl, the twenty-first Azâzêl. And these are the chiefs of their angels and their names, and their chief ones over hundreds and over fifties and over tens]. [4]The name of the first Jeqôn: that is, the one who led astray [all] the sons of God, and brought them [5]down to the earth, and led them astray through the daughters of men. And the second was named Asbeêl: he imparted to the holy sons of God evil counsel, and led them astray so that they defiled [6]their bodies with the daughters of men. And the third was named Gâdreêl: he it is who showed the children of men all the blows of death, and he led astray Eve, and showed [the weapons of death to the sons of men] the shield and the coat of mail, and the sword for battle, and all the weapons [7]of death to the children of men. And from his hand they have proceeded against those who dwell [8]on the earth from that day and forevermore. And the fourth was named Pênêmûe: he taught the [9]children of men the bitter and the sweet, and he taught them all the secrets of their wisdom. And he instructed mankind in writing with ink and paper, and thereby many sinned from eternity to [10]eternity and until this day. For men were not created for such a purpose, to give confirmation [11]to their good faith with pen and ink. For men were created exactly like the angels, to the intent that they should continue pure and righteous, and death, which destroys everything, could not have taken hold of them, but through this their knowledge they are perishing, and through this power [12]it is consuming me. And the fifth was named Kâsdejâ: this is he who showed the children of men all the wicked smitings of spirits and demons, and the smitings of the embryo in the womb, that it may pass away, and [the smitings of the soul] the bites of the serpent, and the smitings [13]which befall through the noontide heat, the son of the serpent named Tabâ'et. And this is the task of Kâsbeêl, the chief of the oath which he showed to the holy ones when he dwelt high [14]above in glory, and its name is Bîqâ. This (angel) requested Michael to show him the hidden name, that he might enunciate it in the oath, so that those might quake before that name and oath who [15]revealed all that was in secret to the children of men. And this is the power of this oath, for it is powerful and strong, and he placed this oath Akâe in the hand of Michael.

[16]And these are the secrets of this oath...
And they are strong through his oath:
And the heaven was suspended before the world was created,
And for ever.

[17]And through it the earth was founded upon the water,

And from the secret recesses of the mountains come beautiful waters,
From the creation of the world and unto eternity.

¹⁸And through that oath the sea was created,
And as its foundation He set for it the sand against the time of (its) anger,
And it dare not pass beyond it from the creation of the world unto eternity.

¹⁹And through that oath are the depths made fast,
And abide and stir not from their place from eternity to eternity.

²⁰And through that oath the sun and moon complete their course,
And deviate not from their ordinance from eternity to eternity.

²¹And through that oath the stars complete their course,
And He calls them by their names,
And they answer Him from eternity to eternity.

²²[And in like manner the spirits of the water, and of the winds, and of all zephyrs, and (their) paths ²³from all the quarters of the winds. And there are preserved the voices of the thunder and the light of the lightnings: and there are preserved the chambers of the hail and the chambers of the ²⁴hoarfrost, and the chambers of the mist, and the chambers of the rain and the dew. And all these believe and give thanks before the Lord of Spirits, and glorify (Him) with all their power, and their food is in every act of thanksgiving: they thank and glorify and extol the name of the Lord of Spirits forever and ever.]

²⁵And this oath is mighty over them
And through it [they are preserved and] their paths are preserved,
And their course is not destroyed.

²⁶And there was great joy amongst them,
And they blessed and glorified and extolled
Because the name of that Son of Man had been revealed unto them.

²⁷And he sat on the throne of his glory,
And the sum of judgment was given unto the Son of Man,
And he caused the sinners to pass away and be destroyed from off the face of the earth,
And those who have led the world astray.

²⁸With chains shall they be bound,
And in their assemblage-place of destruction shall they be imprisoned,
And all their works vanish from the face of the earth.

²⁹And from henceforth there shall be nothing corruptible;

For that Son of Man has appeared,

And has seated himself on the throne of his glory,
And all evil shall pass away before his face,
And the word of that Son of Man shall go forth
And be strong before the Lord of Spirits.

This is the third parable of Enoch.

CHAPTER 70

The Final Translation of Enoch

[1]And it came to pass after this that his name during his lifetime was raised aloft to that Son of [2]Man and to the Lord of Spirits from amongst those who dwell on the earth. And he was raised aloft [3]on the chariots of the spirit and his name vanished among them. And from that day I was no longer numbered amongst them: and he set me between the two winds, between the North and the [4]West, where the angels took the cords to measure for me the place for the elect and righteous. And there I saw the first fathers and the righteous who from the beginning dwell in that place.

CHAPTER 71

Two earlier Visions of Enoch

[1]And it came to pass after this that my spirit was translated
And it ascended into the heavens:
And I saw the holy sons of God.
They were stepping on flames of fire:
Their garments were white [and their raiment],
And their faces shone like snow.

[2]And I saw two streams of fire,
And the light of that fire shone like hyacinth,
And I fell on my face before the Lord of Spirits.

[3]And the angel Michael [one of the archangels] seized me by my right hand,
And lifted me up and led me forth into all the secrets,
And he showed me all the secrets of righteousness.

[4]And he showed me all the secrets of the ends of the heaven,

And all the chambers of all the stars, and all the luminaries,
Whence they proceed before the face of the holy ones.

⁵And he translated my spirit into the heaven of heavens,
And I saw there as it were a structure built of crystals,
And between those crystals tongues of living fire.

⁶And my spirit saw the girdle which girt that house of fire,
And on its four sides were streams full of living fire,
And they girt that house.

⁷And round about were Seraphin, Cherubic, and Ophannin:
And these are they who sleep not
And guard the throne of His glory.

⁸And I saw angels who could not be counted,
A thousand thousands, and ten thousand times ten thousand,
Encircling that house.

And Michael, and Raphael, and Gabriel, and Phanuel,
And the holy angels who are above the heavens,
Go in and out of that house.

⁹And they came forth from that house,
And Michael and Gabriel, Raphael and Phanuel,
And many holy angels without number.

¹⁰And with them the Head of Days,
His head white and pure as wool,
And His raiment indescribable.

¹¹And I fell on my face,
And my whole body became relaxed,
And my spirit was transfigured;

And I cried with a loud voice,
. . . with the spirit of power,
And blessed and glorified and extolled.

¹²And these blessings which went forth out of my mouth were well pleasing before that Head of ¹³Days. And that Head of Days came with Michael and Gabriel, Raphael and Phanuel, thousands and ten thousands of angels without number.

[Lost passage wherein the Son of Man was described as accompanying the Head of Days, and Enoch asked one of the angels (as in 46:3) concerning the Son of Man as to who he was.]

[14] And he (i.e. the angel) came to me and greeted me with His voice, and said unto
me:

'This is the Son of Man who is born unto righteousness,
And righteousness abides over him,
And the righteousness of the Head of Days forsakes him not.'

[15] And he said unto me:
'He proclaims unto thee peace in the name of the world to come;
For from hence has proceeded peace since the creation of the world,
And so shall it be unto thee forever and forever and ever.

[16] And all shall walk in his ways since righteousness never forsaketh him:
With him will be their dwelling-places, and with him their heritage,
And they shall not be separated from him forever and ever and ever.

And so there shall be length of days with that Son of Man,
And the righteous shall have peace and an upright way
In the name of the Lord of Spirits forever and ever.'

Section 3

Chapters 72-82

The Book of the Heavenly Luminaries

CHAPTER 72

The Sun

[1]The book of the courses of the luminaries of the heaven, the relations of each, according to their classes, their dominion and their seasons, according to their names and places of origin, and according to their months, which Uriel, the holy angel, who was with me, who is their guide, showed me; and he showed me all their laws exactly as they are, and how it is with regard to all the years of the world [2]and unto eternity, till the new creation is accomplished which dureth till eternity. And this is the first law of the luminaries: the luminary the Sun has its rising in the eastern portals of the heaven, [3]and its setting in the western portals of the heaven. And I saw six portals in which the sun rises, and six portals in which the sun sets and the moon rises and sets in these portals, and the leaders of the stars and those whom they lead: six in the east and six in the west, and all following each other [4]in accurately corresponding order: also many windows to the right and left of these portals. And first there goes forth the great luminary, named the Sun, and his circumference is like the [5]circumference of the heaven, and he is quite filled with illuminating and heating fire. The chariot on which he ascends, the wind drives, and the sun goes down from the heaven and returns through the north in order to reach the east, and is so guided that he comes to the appropriate (lit. 'that') portal and [6]shines in the face of the heaven. In this way he rises in the first month in the great portal, which [7]is the fourth [those six portals in the cast]. And in that fourth portal from which the sun rises in the first month are twelve window-openings, from which proceed a flame when they are opened in [8]their season. When the sun rises in the heaven, he comes forth through that fourth portal thirty, [9]mornings in succession, and sets accurately in the fourth portal in the west of the heaven. And during this period the day becomes daily longer and the night nightly shorter to the thirtieth [10]morning. On that day the day is longer than the night by a ninth part, and the day amounts exactly to ten parts and the night to eight parts. And the sun rises from that fourth portal, and sets in the fourth and returns to the fifth portal of the east thirty mornings, and rises from it and sets in the fifth [12]portal. And then the day becomes longer by two parts and amounts to eleven parts, and the night [13]becomes shorter and amounts to seven parts. And it returns to the east and enters into the sixth [14]portal, and rises and sets in the sixth portal one-and-thirty mornings on account of its sign. On that day the day becomes longer than the night, and the day becomes double the night, and the day [15]becomes twelve parts, and the night is shortened and becomes six parts. And the sun mounts up to make the day shorter and the night longer, and the sun returns to the east and enters into the [16]sixth portal, and rises from it and sets

thirty mornings. And when thirty mornings are accomplished, [17]the day decreases by exactly one part, and becomes eleven parts, and the night seven. And the sun goes forth from that sixth portal in the west, and goes to the east and rises in the fifth portal for [18]thirty mornings, and sets in the west again in the fifth western portal. On that day the day decreases by two parts, and amounts to ten parts and the night to eight parts. And the sun goes forth from that fifth portal and sets in the fifth portal of the west, and rises in the fourth portal for one-[20]and-thirty mornings on account of its sign, and sets in the west. On that day the day is equalized with the night, [and becomes of equal length], and the night amounts to nine parts and the day to [21]nine parts. And the sun rises from that portal and sets in the west, and returns to the east and rises [22]thirty mornings in the third portal and sets in the west in the third portal. And on that day the night becomes longer than the day, and night becomes longer than night, and day shorter than day till the thirtieth morning, and the night amounts exactly to ten parts and the day to eight [23]parts. And the sun rises from that third portal and sets in the third portal in the west and returns to the east, and for thirty mornings rises [24]in the second portal in the east, and in like manner sets in the second portal in the west of the heaven. And on that day the night amounts to eleven [25]parts and the day to seven parts. And the sun rises on that day from that second portal and sets in the west in the second portal, and returns to the east into the first portal for one-and-thirty [26]mornings, and sets in the first portal in the west of the heaven. And on that day the night becomes longer and amounts to the double of the day: and the night amounts exactly to twelve parts and [27]the day to six. And the sun has (therewith) traversed the divisions of his orbit and turns again on those divisions of his orbit, and enters that portal thirty mornings and sets also in the west [28]opposite to it. And on that night has the night decreased in length by a ninth part, and the night [29]has become eleven parts and the day seven parts. And the sun has returned and entered into the second portal in the east, and returns on those his divisions of his orbit for thirty mornings, rising [30]and setting. And on that day the night decreases in length, and the night amounts to ten parts [31]and the day to eight. And on that day the sun rises from that portal, and sets in the west, and returns to the east, and rises in the third portal for one-and-thirty mornings, and sets in the west of the heaven. [32]On that day the night decreases and amounts to nine parts, and the day to nine parts, and the night [33]is equal to the day and the year is exactly as to its days three hundred and sixty-four. And the length of the day and of the night, and the shortness of the day and of the night arise-through the course [34]of the sun these distinctions are made (lit. 'they are separated'). So it comes that its course becomes [35]daily longer, and its course nightly shorter. And this is the law and the course of the sun, and his return as often as he returns sixty times and rises, i.e. the great luminary which is named the sun, [36]forever and ever. And that which (thus) rises is the great luminary, and is so named according to [37]its appearance, according as the Lord commanded. As he rises, so he sets and decreases not, and rests not, but runs day and night, and his light is sevenfold brighter than that of the moon; but as regards size they are both equal.

CHAPTER 73

The Moon and its Phases

[1]And after this law I saw another law dealing with the smaller luminary, which is named the Moon. [2]And her circumference is like the circumference of the heaven, and her chariot in which she rides [3]is driven by the wind, and light is given to her in (definite) measure. And her rising and setting change every month: and her days are like the days of the sun, and when her light is uniform [4](i.e. full) it amounts to the seventh part of the light of the sun. And thus she rises. And her first phase in the east comes forth on the thirtieth morning: and on that day she becomes visible, and constitutes for you the first phase of the moon on the thirtieth day together with the sun in the [5]portal where the sun rises. And the one half of her goes forth by a seventh part, and her whole circumference is empty, without light, with the exception of one-seventh part of it, (and) the [6]fourteenth part of her light. And when she receives one-seventh part of the half of her light, her light [7]amounts to one-seventh part and the half thereof. And she sets with the sun, and when the sun rises the moon rises with him and receives the half of one part of light, and in that night in the beginning of her morning [in the commencement of the lunar day] the moon sets with the sun, and [8]is invisible that night with the fourteen parts and the half of one of them. And she rises on that day with exactly a seventh part, and comes forth and recedes from the rising of the sun, and in her remaining days she becomes bright in the (remaining) thirteen parts.

CHAPTER 74

The Lunar Year

[1]And I saw another course, a law for her, (and) how according to that law she performs her monthly [2]revolution. And all these Uriel, the holy angel who is the leader of them all, showed to me, and their positions, and I wrote down their positions as he showed them to me, and I wrote down their months [3]as they were, and the appearance of their lights till fifteen days were accomplished. In single seventh parts she accomplishes all her light in the east, and in single seventh parts accomplishes all her [4]darkness in the west. And in certain months she alters her settings, and in certain months she pursues

[5]her own peculiar course. In two months the moon sets with the sun: in those two middle portals the [6]third and the fourth. She goes forth for seven days, and turns about and returns again through the portal where the sun rises, and accomplishes all her light: and she recedes from the sun, and in eight [7]days enters the sixth portal from which the sun goes forth. And when the sun goes forth from the fourth portal she goes forth seven days, until she goes forth from the fifth and turns back again in seven days into the fourth portal and accomplishes all her light: and she recedes and enters into the [8]first portal in eight days. And she returns again in seven days into the fourth portal from which the [9,10]sun goes forth. Thus I saw their position -how the moons rose and the sun set in those days. And if five years are added together the sun has an overplus of thirty days, and all the days which accrue [11]to it for one of those five years, when they are full, amount to 364 days. And the overplus of the sun and of the stars amounts to six days: in 5 years 6 days every year come to 30 days: and the [12]moon falls behind the sun and stars to the number of 30 days. And the sun and the stars bring in all the years exactly, so that they do not advance or delay their position by a single day unto eternity; but complete the years with perfect justice in 364 days. In 3 years there are 1,092 days, and in 5 years 1,820 days, so that in 8 years there are 2,912 days. For the moon alone the days amount in 3 years to 1,062 days, and in 5 years she falls 50 days behind: [i.e. to the sum (of 1,770) there is [15]to be added (1,000 and) 62 days.] And in 5 years there are 1,770 days, so that for the moon the days [16:]in 8 years amount to 2,832 days. [For in 8 years she falls behind to the amount of 80 days], all the [17]days she falls behind in 8 years are 80. And the year is accurately completed in conformity with their world-stations and the stations of the sun, which rise from the portals through which it (the sun) rises and sets 30 days.

CHAPTER 75

[1]And the leaders of the heads of the thousands, who are placed over the whole creation and over all the stars, have also to do with the four intercalary days, being inseparable from their office, according to the reckoning of the year, and these render service on the four days which are not [2]reckoned in the reckoning of the year. And owing to them men go wrong therein, for those luminaries truly render service on the world-stations, one in the first portal, one in the third portal of the heaven, one in the fourth portal, and one in the sixth portal, and the exactness of the year is [3]accomplished through its separate three hundred and sixty-four stations. For the signs and the times and the years and the days the angel Uriel showed to me, whom the Lord of glory hath set for ever over all the luminaries of the heaven, in the heaven and in the world, that they should rule on the face of the heaven and be seen on the earth, and be leaders for the

day and the night, i.e. the sun, moon, and stars, and all the ministering creatures which make their revolution in all the chariots [4]of the heaven. In like manner twelve doors Uriel showed me, open in the circumference of the sun's chariot in the heaven, through which the rays of the sun break forth: and from them is warmth [5]diffused over the earth, when they are opened at their appointed seasons. [And for the winds and [6]the spirit of the dew when they are opened, standing open in the heavens at the ends.] As for the twelve portals in the heaven, at the ends of the earth, out of which go forth the sun, moon, and stars, [7]and all the works of heaven in the east and in the west, There are many windows open to the left and right of them, and one window at its (appointed) season produces warmth, corresponding (as these do) to those doors from which the stars come forth according as He has commanded them, [8]and wherein they set corresponding to their number. And I saw chariots in the heaven, running [9]in the world, above those portals in which revolve the stars that never set. And one is larger than all the rest, and it is that that makes its course through the entire world.

CHAPTER 76

The Twelve Winds and their Portals

[1]And at the ends of the earth I saw twelve portals open to all the quarters (of the heaven), from [2]which the winds go forth and blow over the earth. Three of them are open on the face (i.e. the east) of the heavens, and three in the west, and three on the right (i.e. the south) of the heaven, and [3]three on the left (i.e. the north). And the three first are those of the east, and three are of the [4]north, and three [after those on the left] of the south, and three of the west. Through four of these come winds of blessing and prosperity, and from those eight come hurtful winds: when they are sent, they bring destruction on all the earth and on the water upon it, and on all who dwell thereon, and on everything which is in the water and on the land. [5]And the first wind from those portals, called the east wind, comes forth through the first portal which is in the east, inclining towards the south: from it come forth desolation, drought, heat, [6]and destruction. And through the second portal in the middle comes what is fitting, and from it there come rain and fruitfulness and prosperity and dew; and through the third portal which lies toward the north come cold and drought. [7]And after these come forth the south winds through three portals: through the first portal of [8]them inclining to the east comes forth a hot wind. And through the middle portal next to it there [9]come forth fragrant smells, and dew and rain, and prosperity and health. And through the third portal lying to the west come forth dew and rain, locusts and desolation. [10]And after these the north winds: from the seventh portal in the east come dew and rain,

locusts [11]and desolation. And from the middle portal come in a direct direction health and rain and dew and prosperity; and through the third portal in the west come cloud and hoarfrost, and snow and rain, and dew and locusts. [12]And after these [four] are the west winds: through the first portal adjoining the north come forth [13]dew and hoarfrost, and cold and snow and frost. And from the middle portal come forth dew and rain, and prosperity and blessing; and through the last portal which adjoins the south come forth [14]drought and desolation, and burning and destruction. And the twelve portals of the four quarters of the heaven are therewith completed, and all their laws and all their plagues and all their benefactions have I shown to thee, my son Methuselah.

CHAPTER 77

The Four Quarters of the World: the Seven Mountains, the
Seven Rivers, &c

[1]And the first quarter is called the east, because it is the first: and the second, the south, because the Most High will descend there, yea, there in quite a special sense will He who is blessed forever [2]descend. And the west quarter is named the diminished, because there all the luminaries of the [3]heaven wane and go down. And the fourth quarter, named the north, is divided into three parts: the first of them is for the dwelling of men: and the second contains seas of water, and the abysses and forests and rivers, and darkness and clouds; and the third part contains the garden of righteousness. [4]I saw seven high mountains, higher than all the mountains which are on the earth: and thence [5]comes forth hoarfrost, and days, seasons, and years pass away. I saw seven rivers on the earth larger than all the rivers: one of them coming from the west pours its waters into the Great Sea. [6]And these two come from the north to the sea and pour their waters into the Erythraean Sea in the [7]east. And the remaining, four come forth on the side of the north to their own sea, two of them to the Erythraean Sea, and two into the Great Sea and discharge themselves there [and some say: [8]into the desert]. Seven great islands I saw in the sea and in the mainland: two in the mainland and five in the Great Sea.

CHAPTER 78

The Sun and Moon:
the Waxing and Waning of the Moon

[1,2]And the names of the sun are the following: the first Orjârês, and the second Tômâs. And the moon has four names: the first name is Asônjâ, the second Eblâ, the third Benâsê, and the fourth [3]Erâe. These are the two great luminaries: their circumference is like the circumference of the [4]heaven, and the size of the circumference of both is alike. In the circumference of the sun there are seven portions of light which are added to it more than to the moon, and in definite measures it is [5]transferred till the seventh portion of the sun is exhausted. And they set and enter the portals of the west, and make their revolution by the north, and come forth through the eastern portals [6]on the face of the heaven. And when the moon rises one-fourteenth part appears in the heaven: [7][the light becomes full in her]: on the fourteenth day she accomplishes her light. And fifteen parts of light are transferred to her till the fifteenth day (when) her light is accomplished, according to the sign of the year, and she becomes fifteen parts, and the moon grows by (the addition of) fourteenth [8]parts. And in her waning (the moon) decreases on the first day to fourteen parts of her light, on the second to thirteen parts of light, on the third to twelve, on the fourth to eleven, on the fifth to ten, on the sixth to nine, on the seventh to eight, on the eighth to seven, on the ninth to six, on the tenth to five, on the eleventh to four, on the twelfth to three, on the thirteenth to two, on the fourteenth [9]to the half of a seventh, and all her remaining light disappears wholly on the fifteenth. And [10]in certain months the month has twenty-nine days and once twenty-eight. And Uriel showed me another law: when light is transferred to the moon, and on which side it is transferred to her by [11]the sun. Duringall the period during which the moon is growing in her light, she is transferring it to herself when opposite to the sun during fourteen days [her light is accomplished in the heaven, [12]and when she is illumined throughout, her light is accomplished full in the heaven. And on the first [13]day she is called the new moon, for on that day the light rises upon her. She becomes full moon exactly on the day when the sun sets in the west, and from the east she rises at night, and the moon shines the whole night through till the sun rises over against her and the moon is seen over against [14]the sun. On the side whence the light of the moon comes forth, there again she wanes till all the light vanishes and all the days of the month are at an end, and her circumference is empty, void of [15]light. And three months she makes of thirty days, and at her time she makes three months of twenty-nine days each, in which she accomplishes her waning in the first period of time, and in the first [16]portal for one hundred and seventy-seven days. And in the time of her going out she appears for three months (of) thirty days each,

and for three months she appears (of) twenty-nine each. At night she appears like a man for twenty days each time, and by day she appears like the heaven, and there is nothing else in her save her light.

Chapters 79-80

Recapitulation of several of the Laws

CHAPTER 79

[1]And now, my son, I have shown thee everything, and the law of all the stars of the heaven is [2]completed. And he showed me all the laws of these for every day, and for every season of bearing rule, and for every year, and for its going forth, and for the order prescribed to it every month [3]and every week: And the waning of the moon which takes place in the sixth portal: for in this [4]sixth portal her light is accomplished, and after that there is the beginning of the waning: (And the waning) which takes place in the first portal in its season, till one hundred and seventy-seven [5]days are accomplished: reckoned according to weeks, twenty-five (weeks) and two days. She falls behind the sun and the order of the stars exactly five days in the course of one period, and when [6]this place which thou seest has been traversed. Such is the picture and sketch of every luminary which Uriel the archangel, who is their leader, showed unto me.

CHAPTER 80

[1]And in those days the angel Uriel answered and said to me: 'Behold, I have shown thee everything, Enoch, and I have revealed everything to thee that thou shouldst see this sun and this moon, and the leaders of the stars of the heaven and all those who turn them, their tasks and times and departures.

Chapter 80:2-8

*Perversion of Nature and the heavenly Bodies due to the Sin
of Men*

[2]And in the days of the sinners the years shall be shortened,
And their seed shall be tardy on their lands and fields,
And all things on the earth shall alter,

And shall not appear in their time:
And the rain shall be kept back
And the heaven shall withhold (it).

[3]And in those times the fruits of the earth shall be backward,
And shall not grow in their time,
And the fruits of the trees shall be withheld in their time.

[4]And the moon shall alter her order,
And not appear at her time.

[5][And in those days the sun shall be seen and he shall journey in the evening on the extremity of the great chariot in the west]

And shall shine more brightly than accords with the order of light.

[6]And many chiefs of the stars shall transgress the order (prescribed).
And these shall alter their orbits and tasks,
And not appear at the seasons prescribed to them.

[7]And the whole order of the stars shall be concealed from the sinners,
And the thoughts of those on the earth shall err concerning them,
[And they shall be altered from all their ways],
Yea, they shall err and take them to be gods.

[8]And evil shall be multiplied upon them,
And punishment shall come upon them So as to destroy all.'

CHAPTER 81

The Heavenly Tablets and the Mission of Enoch

[1]And he said unto me:
'Observe, Enoch, these heavenly tablets,
And read what is written thereon,
And mark every individual fact.'

[2]And I observed the heavenly tablets, and read everything which was written (thereon) and understood everything, and read the book of all the deeds of mankind, and of all the children of flesh [3]that shall be upon the earth to the remotest generations. And

forthwith I blessed the great Lord the King of glory forever, in that He has made all the works of the world,

> And I extolled the Lord because of His patience,
> And blessed Him because of the children of men.

⁴ And after that I said:
'Blessed is the man who dies in righteousness and goodness,
Concerning whom there is no book of unrighteousness written,
And against whom no day of judgment shall be found.'

⁵And those seven holy ones brought me and placed me on the earth before the door of my house, and said to me: 'Declare everything to thy son Methuselah, and show to all thy children that no ⁶flesh is righteous in the sight of the Lord, for He is their Creator. One year we will leave thee with thy son, till thou givest thy (last) commands, that thou mayest teach thy children and record (it) for them, and testify to all thy children; and in the second year they shall take thee from their midst.

> ⁷Let thy heart be strong,
> For the good shall announce righteousness to the good;

> The righteous with the righteous shall rejoice,
> And shall offer congratulation to one another.

> ⁸But the sinners shall die with the sinners,
> And the apostate go down with the apostate.

> ⁹And those who practice righteousness shall die on account of the deeds of men,
> And be taken away on account of the doings of the godless.'

¹⁰And in those days they ceased to speak to me, and I came to my people, blessing the Lord of the world.

CHAPTER 82

Charge given to Enoch: the four Intercalary days: the Stars
which lead the Seasons and the Months

¹And now, my son Methuselah, all these things I am recounting to thee and writing down for thee! and I have revealed to thee everything, and given thee books concerning all these: so preserve, my son Methuselah, the books from thy father's hand, and (see) that thou deliver them to the generations of the world.

> ²I have given wisdom to thee and to thy children,

[And thy children that shall be to thee],
That they may give it to their children for generations,
This wisdom (namely) that passeth their thought.

[3]And those who understand it shall not sleep,
But shall listen with the ear that they may learn this wisdom,
And it shall please those that eat thereof better than good food.

[4]Blessêd are all the righteous, blessed are all those who walk in the way of righteousness and sin not as the sinners, in the reckoning of all their days in which the sun traverses t he heaven, entering into and departing from the portals for thirty days with the heads of thousands of the order of the stars, together with the four which are intercalated which divide the four portions of the year, which [5]lead them and enter with them four days. Owing to them men shall be at fault and not reckon them in the whole reckoning of the year: yea, men shall be at fault, and not recognize them accurately. [6]For they belong to the reckoning of the year and are truly recorded (thereon) forever, one in the first portal and one in the third, and one in the fourth and one in the sixth, and the year is completed in three hundred and sixty-four days. [7]And the account thereof is accurate and the recorded reckoning thereof exact; for the luminaries, and months and festivals, and years and days, has Uriel shown and revealed to me, to whom the [8]Lord of the whole creation of the world hath subjected the host of heaven. And he has power over night and day in the heaven to cause the light to give light to men -sun, moon, and stars, [9]and all the powers of the heaven which revolve in their circular chariots. And these are the orders of the stars, which set in their places, and in their seasons and festivals and months. [10]And these are the names of those who lead them, who watch that they enter at their times, in their orders, in their seasons, in their months, in their periods of dominion, and in their positions. [11]Their four leaders who divide the four parts of the year enter first; and after them the twelve leaders of the orders who divide the months; and for the three hundred and sixty (days) there are heads over thousands who divide the days; and for the four intercalary days there are the leaders which sunder [12]the four parts of the year. And these heads over thousands are intercalated between [13]leader and leader, each behind a station, but their leaders make the division. And these are the names of the leaders who divide the four parts of the year which are ordained: Mîlkî'êl, Hel'emmêlêk, and Mêl'êjal, [14]and Nârêl. And the names of those who lead them: Adnâr'êl, and Ijâsûsa'êl, and 'Elômê'êl -these three follow the leaders of the orders, and there is one that follows the three leaders of the orders which follow those leaders of stations that divide the four parts of the year. [15]In the beginning of the year Melkejâl rises first and rules, who is named Tam'âinî and sun, and [16]all the days of his dominion whilst he bears rule are ninety-one days. And these are the signs of the days which are to be seen on earth in the days of his dominion: sweat, and heat, and calms; and all the trees bear fruit, and leaves are produced on all the trees, and the harvest of

wheat, and the rose-flowers, and all the flowers which come forth in the field, but the trees of the winter season [17]become withered. And these are the names of the leaders which are under them: Berka'êl, Zêlebs'êl, and another who is added a head of a thousand, called Hîlûjâseph: and the days of the dominion of this (leader) are at an end. [18]The next leader after him is Hêl'emmêlêk, whom one names the shining sun, and all the days [19]of his light are ninety-one days. And these are the signs of (his) days on the earth: glowing heat and dryness, and the trees ripen their fruits and produce all their fruits ripe and ready, and the sheep pair and become pregnant, and all the fruits of the earth are gathered in, and everything that is [20]in the fields, and the winepress: these things take place in the days of his dominion. These are the names, and the orders, and the leaders of those heads of thousands: Gîdâ'îjal, Kê'êl, and Hê'êl, and the name of the head of a thousand which is added to them, Asfâ'êl: and the days of his dominion are at an end.

Section 4

Chapters 83-90

The Dream-Visions

Chapters 83-84

First Dream-Vision on the Deluge

CHAPTER 83

[1]And now, my son Methuselah, I will show thee all my visions which I have seen, recounting [2]them before thee. Two visions I saw before I took a wife, and the one was quite unlike the other: the first when I was learning to write: the second before I took thy mother, (when) I saw a terrible [3]vision. And regarding them I prayed to the Lord. I had laid me down in the house of my grandfather Mahalalel, (when) I saw in a vision how the heaven collapsed and was borne off and fell to [4]the earth. And when it fell to the earth I saw how the earth was swallowed up in a great abyss, and mountains were suspended on mountains, and hills sank down on hills, and high trees were rent [5]from their stems, and hurled down and sunk in the abyss. And thereupon a word fell into my mouth, [6]and I lifted up (my voice) to cry aloud, and said: 'The earth is destroyed.' And my grandfather Mahalalel waked me as I lay near him, and said unto me: 'Why dost thou cry so, my son, and why [7]dost thou make such lamentation?' And I recounted to him the whole vision which I had seen, and he said unto me: 'A terrible thing hast thou seen, my son, and of grave moment is thy dream-vision as to the secrets of all the sin of the earth: it must sink into the abyss and be destroyed with [8]a great destruction. And now, my son, arise and make petition to the Lord of glory, since thou art a believer, that a remnant may remain on the earth, and that He may not destroy the whole [9]earth. My son, from heaven all this will come upon the earth, and upon the earth there will be great [10]destruction. After that I arose and prayed and implored and besought, and wrote down my prayer [11]for the generations of the world, and I will show everything to thee, my son Methuselah. And when I had gone forth below and seen the heaven, and the sun rising in the east, and the moon setting in the west, and a few stars, and the whole earth, and everything as He had known it in the beginning, then I blessed the Lord of judgment and extolled Him because He had made the sun to go forth from the windows of the east, and he ascended and rose on the face of the heaven, and set out and kept traversing the path shown unto him.

CHAPTER 84

[1]And I lifted up my hands in righteousness and blessed the Holy and Great One, and spake with the breath of my mouth, and with the tongue of flesh, which God has made for the children of the flesh of men, that they should speak therewith, and He gave them breath and a tongue and a mouth that they should speak therewith:

[2]'Blessed be Thou, O Lord, King,
Great and mighty in Thy greatness,
Lord of the whole creation of the heaven,
King of kings and God of the whole world.

And Thy power and kingship and greatness abide forever and ever,
And throughout all generations Thy dominion;
And all the heavens are Thy throne forever,
And the whole earth Thy footstool forever and ever.

[3]For Thou hast made and Thou rulest all things,
And nothing is too hard for Thee,
Wisdom departs not from the place of Thy throne,
Nor turns away from Thy presence.
And Thou knowest and seest and hearest everything,
And there is nothing hidden from Thee [for Thou seest everything].

[4]And now the angels of Thy heavens are guilty of trespass,
And upon the flesh of men abideth Thy wrath until the great day of judgment.

[5]And now, O God and Lord and Great King,
I implore and beseech Thee to fulfill my prayer,
To leave me a posterity on earth,
And not destroy all the flesh of man,
And make the earth without inhabitant,
So that there should be an eternal destruction.

[6]And now, my Lord, destroy from the earth the flesh which has aroused Thy wrath,
But the flesh of righteousness and uprightness establish as a plant of the eternal seed,
And hide not Thy face from the prayer of Thy servant, O Lord.'

Chapters 85-90

Second Dream-Vision of Enoch:
the History of the World to the Founding of the Messianic
Kingdom

CHAPTER 85

[1,2]And after this I saw another dream, and I will show the whole dream to thee, my son. And Enoch lifted up (his voice) and spake to his son Methuselah: 'To thee, my son, will I speak: hear my [3]words -incline thine ear to the dream-vision of thy father. Before I took thy mother Edna, I saw in a vision on my bed, and behold a bull came forth from the earth, and that bull was white; and after it came forth a heifer, and along with this (latter) came forth two bulls, one of them black and [4]the other red. And that black bull gored the red one and pursued him over the earth, and thereupon [5]I could no longer see that red bull. But that black bull grew and that heifer went with him, and [6]I saw that many oxen proceeded from him which resembled and followed him. And that cow, that first one, went from the presence of that first bull in order to seek that red one, but found him [7]not, and lamented with a great lamentation over him and sought him. And I looked till that first [8]bull came to her and quieted her, and from that time onward she cried no more. And after that she bore another white bull, and after him she bore many bulls and black cows. [9]And I saw in my sleep that white bull likewise grow and become a great white bull, and from Him proceeded many white bulls, and they resembled him. And they began to beget many white bulls, which resembled them, one following the other, (even) many.

CHAPTER 86

The Fall of the Angels and the Demoralization of Mankind

[1]And again I saw with mine eyes as I slept, and I saw the heaven above, and behold a star fell [2]from heaven, and it arose and eat and pastured amongst those oxen. And after that I saw the large and the black oxen, and behold they all changed their stalls and pastures and their cattle, and began [3]to live with each other. And again I saw in the vision, and looked towards the heaven, and behold I saw many stars descend and cast themselves down from heaven to that first star, and they became [4]bulls amongst those cattle and pastured with them [amongst them]. And I looked at them and saw, and

behold they all let out their privy members, like horses, and began to cover the cows of the oxen, [5]and they all became pregnant and bare elephants, camels, and asses. And all the oxen feared them and were affrighted at them, and began to bite with their teeth and to devour, and to gore with their [6]horns. And they began, moreover, to devour those oxen; and behold all the children of the earth began to tremble and quake before them and to flee from them.

CHAPTER 87

The Advent of the Seven Archangels

[1]And again I saw how they began to gore each other and to devour each other, and the earth [2]began to cry aloud. And I raised mine eyes again to heaven, and I saw in the vision, and behold there came forth from heaven beings who were like white men: and four went forth from that place [3]and three with them. And those three that had last come forth grasped me by my hand and took me up, away from the generations of the earth, and raised me up to a lofty place, and showed me [4]a tower raised high above the earth, and all the hills were lower. And one said unto me: 'Remain here till thou seest everything that befalls those elephants, camels, and asses, and the stars and the oxen, and all of them.'

CHAPTER 88

The Punishment of the Fallen Angels by the Archangels

[1]And I saw one of those four who had come forth first, and he seized that first star which had fallen from the heaven, and bound it hand and foot and cast it into an abyss: now that abyss was [2]narrow and deep, and horrible and dark. And one of them drew a sword, and gave it to those elephants and camels and asses: then they began to smite each other, and the whole earth quaked [3]because of them. And as I was beholding in the vision, lo, one of those four who had come forth stoned (them) from heaven, and gathered and took all the great stars whose privy members were like those of horses, and bound them all hand and foot, and cast them in an abyss of the earth.

CHAPTER 89

(89:1-9) The Deluge and the Deliverance of Noah

¹And one of those four went to that white bull and instructed him in a secret, without his being terrified: he was born a bull and became a man, and built for himself a great vessel and dwelt thereon; ²and three bulls dwelt with him in that vessel and they were covered in. And again I raised mine eyes towards heaven and saw a lofty roof, with seven water torrents thereon, and those torrents ³flowed with much water into an enclosure. And I saw again, and behold fountains were opened on the surface of that great enclosure, and that water began to swell and rise upon the surface, ⁴and I saw that enclosure till all its surface was covered with water. And the water, the darkness, and mist increased upon it; and as I looked at the height of that water, that water had risen above the height of that enclosure, and was streaming over that enclosure, and it stood upon the earth. ⁵And all the cattle of that enclosure were gathered together until I saw how they sank and were ⁶swallowed up and perished in that water. But that vessel floated on the water, while all the oxen and elephants and camels and asses sank to the bottom with all the animals, so that I could no longer ⁷see them, and they were not able to escape, (but) perished and sank into the depths. And again I saw in the vision till those water torrents were removed from that high roof, and the chasms ⁸of the earth were leveled up and other abysses were opened. Then the water began to run down into these, till the earth became visible; but that vessel settled on the earth, and the darkness ⁹retired and light appeared. But that white bull which had become a man came out of that vessel, and the three bulls with him, and one of those three was white like that bull, and one of them was red as blood, and one black: and that white bull departed from them.

(89:10-27) From the Death of Noah to the Exodus

¹⁰And they began to bring forth beasts of the field and birds, so that there arose different genera: lions, tigers, wolves, dogs, hyenas, wild boars, foxes, squirrels, swine, falcons, vultures, kites, ¹¹eagles, and ravens; and among them was born a white bull. And they began to bite one another; but that white bull which was born amongst them begat a wild ass and a white bull with it, and the ¹²wild asses multiplied. But that bull which was born from him begat a black wild boar and a white ¹³sheep; and the former begat many boars, but that sheep begat twelve sheep. And when those twelve sheep had grown, they gave up one of them to the asses, and those asses again gave up that sheep ¹⁴to the wolves, and that sheep grew up among the wolves. And the Lord brought the eleven sheep to live with it and to pasture with it among the wolves: and they

multiplied and became many [15]flocks of sheep. And the wolves began to fear them, and they oppressed them until they destroyed their little ones, and they cast their young into a river of much water: but those sheep began to [16]cry aloud on account of their little ones, and to complain unto their Lord. And a sheep which had been saved from the wolves fled and escaped to the wild asses; and I saw the sheep how they lamented and cried, and besought their Lord with all their might, till that Lord of the sheep descended [17]at the voice of the sheep from a lofty abode, and came to them and pastured them. And He called that sheep which had escaped the wolves, and spake with it concerning the wolves that it should [18]admonish them not to touch the sheep. And the sheep went to the wolves according to the word of the Lord, and another sheep met it and went with it, and the two went and entered together into the assembly of those wolves, and spake with them and admonished them not to touch the [19]sheep from henceforth. And thereupon I saw the wolves, and how they oppressed the sheep [20]exceedingly with all their power; and the sheep cried aloud. And the Lord came to the sheep and they began to smite those wolves: and the wolves began to make lamentation; but the sheep became [21]quiet and forthwith ceased to cry out. And I saw the sheep till they departed from amongst the wolves; but the eyes of the wolves were blinded, and those wolves departed in pursuit of the sheep [22]with all their power. And the Lord of the sheep went with them, as their leader, and all His sheep [23]followed Him: and his face was dazzling and glorious and terrible to behold. But the wolves [24]began to pursue those sheep till they reached a sea of water. And that sea was divided, and the water stood on this side and on that before their face, and their Lord led them and placed Himself between [25]them and the wolves. And as those wolves did not yet see the sheep, they proceeded into the midst of that sea, and the wolves followed the sheep, and [those wolves] ran after them into that sea. [26]And when they saw the Lord of the sheep, they turned to flee before His face, but that sea gathered itself together, and became as it had been created, and the water swelled and rose till it covered [27]those wolves. And I saw till all the wolves who pursued those sheep perished and were drowned.

(89:28-40) Israel in the Desert, the Giving of the Law, the Entrance into Palestine

[28]But the sheep escaped from that water and went forth into a wilderness, where there was no water and no grass; and they began to open their eyes and to see; and I saw the Lord of the sheep [29]pasturing them and giving them water and grass, and that sheep going and leading them. And that [30]sheep ascended to the summit of that lofty rock, and the Lord of the sheep sent it to them. And after that I saw the Lord of the sheep who stood before them, and His appearance was great and [31]terrible and majestic, and

all those sheep saw Him and were afraid before His face. And they all feared and trembled because of Him, and they cried to that sheep with them [which was amongst [31]them]: 'We are not able to stand before our Lord or to behold Him.' And that sheep which led them again ascended to the summit of that rock, but the sheep began to be blinded and to wander [33]from the way which he had showed them, but that sheep wot not thereof. And the Lord of the sheep was wrathful exceedingly against them, and that sheep discovered it, and went down from the summit of the rock, and came to the sheep, and found the greatest part of them blinded and fallen [34]away. And when they saw it they feared and trembled at its presence, and desired to return to their [35]folds. And that sheep took other sheep with it, and came to those sheep which had fallen away, and began to slay them; and the sheep feared its presence, and thus that sheep brought back those [36]sheep that had fallen away, and they returned to their folds. And I saw in this vision till that sheep became a man and built a house for the Lord of the sheep, and placed all the sheep in that house. [37]And I saw till this sheep which had met that sheep which led them fell asleep: and I saw till all the great sheep perished and little ones arose in their place, and they came to a pasture, and [38]approached a stream of water. Then that sheep, their leader which had become a man, withdrew [39]from them and fell asleep, and all the sheep sought it and cried over it with a great crying. And I saw till they left off crying for that sheep and crossed that stream of water, and there arose the two sheep as leaders in the place of those which had led them and fallen asleep (lit. 'had fallen asleep and led [40]them'). And I saw till the sheep came to a goodly place, and a pleasant and glorious land, and I saw till those sheep were satisfied; and that house stood amongst them in the pleasant land.

(89:41-50) From the Time of the Judges to the Building of the Temple

[41]And sometimes their eyes were opened, and sometimes blinded, till another sheep arose and led them and brought them all back, and their eyes were opened. [42]And the dogs and the foxes and the wild boars began to devour those sheep till the Lord of the sheep raised up [another sheep] a ram from their [43]midst, which led them. And that ram began to butt on either side those dogs, foxes, and wild [44]boars till he had destroyed them all. And that sheep whose eyes were opened saw that ram, which was amongst the sheep, till it forsook its glory and began to butt those sheep, and trampled upon them, and behaved itself [45]unseemly. And the Lord of the sheep sent the lamb to another lamb and raised it to being a ram and leader of the sheep instead of that [46]ram which had forsaken its glory. And it went to it and spake to it alone, and raised it to being a ram, and made it the prince and leader of the sheep; but during all these things those dogs [47]oppressed the sheep. And the first ram pursued that second ram, and that

second ram arose and fled before it; and I saw till those dogs pulled [48]down the first ram. And that second ram arose [49]and led the [little] sheep. And those sheep grew and multiplied; but all the dogs, and foxes, and wild boars feared and fled before it, and that ram butted and killed the wild beasts, and those wild beasts had no longer any power among the [48b]sheep and robbed them no more of ought. And that ram begat many sheep and fell asleep; and a little sheep became ram in its stead, and became prince and leader of those sheep. [50]And that house became great and broad, and it was built for those sheep: (and) a tower lofty and great was built on the house for the Lord of the sheep, and that house was low, but the tower was elevated and lofty, and the Lord of the sheep stood on that tower and they offered a full table before Him.

(89:51-67) The Two Kingdoms of Israel and Judah to the Destruction of Jerusalem

[51]And again I saw those sheep that they again erred and went many ways, and forsook that their house, and the Lord of the sheep called some from amongst the sheep and sent them to the sheep, [52]but the sheep began to slay them. And one of them was saved and was not slain, and it sped away and cried aloud over the sheep; and they sought to slay it, but the Lord of the sheep saved it from [53]the sheep, and brought it up to me, and caused it to dwell there. And many other sheep He sent [54]to those sheep to testify unto them and lament over them. And after that I saw that when they forsook the house of the Lord and His tower they fell away entirely, and their eyes were blinded; and I saw the Lord of the sheep how He wrought much slaughter amongst them in their herds until [55]those sheep invited that slaughter and betrayed His place. And He gave them over into the hands of the lions and tigers, and wolves and hyenas, and into the hand of the foxes, and to all the wild [56]beasts, and those wild beasts began to tear in pieces those sheep. And I saw that He forsook that their house and their tower and gave them all into the hand of the lions, to tear and devour them, [57]into the hand of all the wild beasts. And I began to cry aloud with all my power, and to appeal to the Lord of the sheep, and to represent to Him in regard to the sheep that they were devoured [58]by all the wild beasts. But He remained unmoved, though He saw it, and rejoiced that they were devoured and swallowed and robbed, and left them to be devoured in the hand of all the beasts. [59]And He called seventy shepherds, and cast those sheep to them that they might pasture them, and He spake to the shepherds and their companions: 'Let each individual of you pasture the sheep [60]henceforward, and everything that I shall command you that do ye. And I will deliver them over unto you duly numbered, and tell you which of them are to be destroyed-and them destroy ye.' And [61]He gave over unto them those sheep. And He called another and spake unto him: 'Observe and mark everything that the shepherds will do to those sheep; for they will destroy more of

them than [62]I have commanded them. And every excess and the destruction which will be wrought through the shepherds, record (namely) how many they destroy according to my command, and how many according to their own caprice: record against every individual shepherd all the destruction he [63]effects. And read out before me by number how many they destroy, and how many they deliver over for destruction, that I may have this as a testimony against them, and know every deed of the shepherds, that I may comprehend and see what they do, whether or not they abide by my [64]command which I have commanded them. But they shall not know it, and thou shalt not declare it to them, nor admonish them, but only record against each individual all the destruction which [65]the shepherds effect each in his time and lay it all before me.' And I saw till those shepherds pastured in their season, and they began to slay and to destroy more than they were bidden, and they delivered [66]those sheep into the hand of the lions. And the lions and tigers eat and devoured the greater part of those sheep, and the wild boars eat along with them; and they burnt that tower and demolished [67]that house. And I became exceedingly sorrowful over that tower because that house of the sheep was demolished, and afterwards I was unable to see if those sheep entered that house.

(89:68-71) First Period of the Angelic Rulers -from the Destruction of Jerusalem to the Return from Captivity

[68]And the shepherds and their associates delivered over those sheep to all the wild beasts, to devour them, and each one of them received in his time a definite number: it was written by the other [69]in a book how many each one of them destroyed of them. And each one slew and destroyed many [70]more than was prescribed; and I began to weep and lament on account of those sheep. And thus in the vision I saw that one who wrote, how he wrote down every one that was destroyed by those shepherds, day by day, and carried up and laid down and showed actually the whole book to the Lord of the sheep-(even) everything that they had done, and all that each one of them had made [71]away with, and all that they had given over to destruction. And the book was read before the Lord of the sheep, and He took the book from his hand and read it and sealed it and laid it down.

(89:72-77) Second Period -from the Time of Cyrus to that of Alexander the Great

[72]And forthwith I saw how the shepherds pastured for twelve hours, and behold three of those sheep turned back and came and entered and began to build up all that had fallen down of that [73]house; but the wild boars tried to hinder them, but they were not able. And they began again to build as before, and they reared up that tower, and it was

named the high tower; and they began again to place a table before the tower, but all the bread on it was polluted and not pure. [74]And as touching all this the eyes of those sheep were blinded so that they saw not, and (the eyes of) their shepherds likewise; and they delivered them in large numbers to their shepherds for [75]destruction, and they trampled the sheep with their feet and devoured them. And the Lord of the sheep remained unmoved till all the sheep were dispersed over the field and mingled with them (i.e. the [76]beasts), and they (i.e. the shepherds) did not save them out of the hand of the beasts. And this one who wrote the book carried it up, and showed it and read it before the Lord of the sheep, and implored Him on their account, and besought Him on their account as he showed Him all the doings [77]of the shepherds, and gave testimony before Him against all the shepherds. And he took the actual book and laid it down beside Him and departed.

(90:1-5) Third Period -from Alexander the Great to the Graeco-Syrian Domination

CHAPTER 90

[1]And I saw till that in this manner thirty-five shepherds undertook the pasturing (of the sheep), and they severally completed their periods as did the first; and others received them into their [2]hands, to pasture them for their period, each shepherd in his own period. And after that I saw in my vision all the birds of heaven coming, the eagles, the vultures, the kites, the ravens; but the eagles led all the birds; and they began to devour those sheep, and to pick out their eyes and to [3]devour their flesh. And the sheep cried out because their flesh was being devoured by the birds, [4]and as for me I looked and lamented in my sleep over that shepherd who pastured the sheep. And I saw until those sheep were devoured by the dogs and eagles and kites, and they left neither flesh nor skin nor sinew remaining on them till only their bones stood there: and their bones too fell [5]to the earth and the sheep became few. And I saw until that twenty-three had undertaken the pasturing and completed in their several periods fifty-eight times.

(90:6-12) Fourth Period -from the Graeco-Syrian Domination to the Maccabean Revolt

[6]But behold lambs were borne by those white sheep, and they began to open their eyes and to see, [7]and to cry to the sheep. Yea, they cried to them, but they did not hearken to what they said to [8]them, but were exceedingly deaf, and their eyes were very

exceedingly blinded. And I saw in the vision how the ravens flew upon those lambs and took one of those lambs, and dashed the sheep [9]in pieces and devoured them. And I saw till horns grew upon those lambs, and the ravens cast down their horns; and I saw till there sprouted a great horn of one of those sheep, and their eyes [10]were opened. And it looked at them [and their eyes opened], and it cried to the sheep, and the [11]rams saw it and all ran to it. And notwithstanding all this those eagles and vultures and ravens and kites still kept tearing the sheep and swooping down upon them and devouring them: still the [12]sheep remained silent, but the rams lamented and cried out. And those ravens fought and battled with it and sought to lay low its horn, but they had no power over it.

(90:13-19) The last Assault of the Gentiles on the Jews
(where vv. 13-15 and 16-18 are doublets)

[13]And I saw till the shepherds and eagles and those vultures and kites came, and they cried to the ravens that they should break the horn of that ram, and they battled and fought with it, and it battled with them and cried that its help might come. [14]And I saw till that man, who wrote down the names of the shepherds [and] carried up into the presence of the Lord of the sheep [came and helped it and showed it everything: he had come down for the help of that ram]. [15]And I saw till the Lord of the sheep came unto them in wrath, and all who saw Him fled, and they all fell into His shadow from before His face. [16]All the eagles and vultures and ravens and kites were gathered together, and there came with them all the sheep of the field, yea, they all came together, and helped each other to break that horn of the ram. [17]And I saw that man, who wrote the book according to the command of the Lord, till he opened that book concerning the destruction which those twelve last shepherds had wrought, and showed that they had destroyed much more than their predecessors, before the Lord of the sheep. [18]And I saw till the Lord of the sheep came unto them and took in His hand the staff of His wrath, and smote the earth, and the earth clave asunder, and all the beasts and all the birds of the heaven fell from among those sheep, and were swallowed up in the earth and it covered them. [19]And I saw till a great sword was given to the sheep, and the sheep proceeded against all the beasts of the field to slay them, and all the beasts and the birds of the heaven fled before their face.

(90:20-27) Judgment of the Fallen Angels, the Shepherds,
and the Apostates

[20]And I saw till a throne was erected in the pleasant land, and the Lord of the sheep sat Himself thereon, and the other took the sealed books and opened those books before

the Lord of the sheep. [21]And the Lord called those men the seven first white ones, and commanded that they should bring before Him, beginning with the first star which led the way, all the stars whose privy members [22]were like those of horses, and they brought them all before Him. And He said to that man who wrote before Him, being one of those seven white ones, and said unto him: 'Take those seventy shepherds to whom I delivered the sheep, and who taking them on their own authority slew more [23]than I commanded them.' And behold they were all bound, I saw, and they all stood before Him. [24]And the judgment was held first over the stars, and they were judged and found guilty, and went to the place of condemnation, and they were cast into an abyss, full of fire and flaming, and full [25]of pillars of fire. And those seventy shepherds were judged and found guilty, and they were cast [26]into that fiery abyss. And I saw at that time how a like abyss was opened in the midst of the earth, full of fire, and they brought those blinded sheep, and they were all judged and found guilty and [27]cast into this fiery abyss, and they burned; now this abyss was to the right of that house. And I saw those sheep burning and their bones burning.

(90:28-42) The New Jerusalem, the Conversion of the
surviving Gentiles, the Resurrection of the Righteous, the
Messiah; Enoch awakes and weeps

[28]And I stood up to see till they folded up that old house; and carried off all the pillars, and all the beams and ornaments of the house were at the same time folded up with it, and they carried [29]it off and laid it in a place in the south of the land. And I saw till the Lord of the sheep brought a new house greater and loftier than that first, and set it up in the place of the first which had beer folded up: all its pillars were new, and its ornaments were new and larger than those of the first, the old one which He had taken away, and all the sheep were within it. [30]And I saw all the sheep which had been left, and all the beasts on the earth, and all the birds of the heaven, falling down and doing homage to those sheep and making petition to and obeying [31]them in everything. And thereafter those three who were clothed in white and had seized me by my hand [who had taken me up before], and the hand of that ram also seizing hold of me, they [32]took me up and set me down in the midst of those sheep before the judgment took place. And those [33]sheep were all white, and their wool was abundant and clean. And all that had been destroyed and dispersed, and all the beasts of the field, and all the birds of the heaven, assembled in that house, and the Lord of the sheep rejoiced with great joy because they were all good and had returned to [34]His house. And I saw till they laid down that sword, which had been given to the sheep, and they brought it back into the house, and it was sealed before the presence of the Lord, and all the sheep [35]were invited into that house, but it held them not. And the eyes of them all were opened, and

they [36]saw the good, and there was not one among them that did not see. And I saw that that house was large and broad and very full. [37]And I saw that a white bull was born, with large horns and all the beasts of the field and all the [38]birds of the air feared him and made petition to him all the time. And I saw till all their generations were transformed, and they all became white bulls; and the first among them became a lamb, and that lamb became a great animal and had great black horns on its head; and the Lord of the sheep [39]rejoiced over it and over all the oxen. And I slept in their midst: and I awoke and saw everything. [40]This is the vision which I saw while I slept, and I awoke and blessed the Lord of righteousness and [41]gave Him glory. Then I wept with a great weeping and my tears stayed not till I could no longer endure it: when I saw, they flowed on account of what I had seen; for everything shall come and [42]be fulfilled, and all the deeds of men in their order were shown to me. On that night I remembered the first dream, and because of it I wept and was troubled-because I had seen that vision.

Section 5

Chapters 91-104 (i.e. 92, 91:1-1O, 18-19, 93:1-1O, 91:12-17, 94-104.)

A Book of Exhortation and Promised Blessing for
the Righteous and of Malediction
and Woe for the Sinners

Chapter 91:1-10, 18-19

Enoch's Admonition to his Children

CHAPTER 91

¹'And now, my son Methuselah, call to me all thy brothers
And gather together to me all the sons of thy mother;
For the word calls me,
And the spirit is poured out upon me,
That I may show you everything
That shall befall you forever.'

²And thereupon Methuselah went and summoned to him all his brothers and assembled his relatives.

³And he spake unto all the children of righteousness and said:

'Hear, ye sons of Enoch, all the words of your father,
And hearken aright to the voice of my mouth;
For I exhort you and say unto you, beloved:

⁴Love uprightness and walk therein.
And draw not nigh to uprightness with a double heart,
And associate not with those of a double heart,

But walk in righteousness, my sons.
And it shall guide you on good paths,
And righteousness shall be your companion.

⁵For I know that violence must increase on the earth,
And a great chastisement be executed on the earth,
And all unrighteousness come to an end:

Yea, it shall be cut off from its roots,
And its whole structure be destroyed.

⁶And unrighteousness shall again be consummated on the earth,
And all the deeds of unrighteousness and of violence
And transgression shall prevail in a twofold degree.

⁷And when sin and unrighteousness and blasphemy

And violence in all kinds of deeds increase,
And apostasy and transgression and uncleanness increase,

A great chastisement shall come from heaven upon all these,
And the holy Lord will come forth with wrath and chastisement
To execute judgment on earth.

[8]In those days violence shall be cut off from its roots,
And the roots of unrighteousness together with deceit,
And they shall be destroyed from under heaven.

[9]And all the idols of the heathen shall be abandoned,
And the temples burned with fire,
And they shall remove them from the whole earth,

And they (i.e. the heathen) shall be cast into the judgment of fire,
And shall perish in wrath and in grievous judgment for ever.

[10]And the righteous shall arise from their sleep,
And wisdom shall arise and be given unto them.

[11][And after that the roots of unrighteousness shall be cut off, and the sinners shall be destroyed by the sword ... shall be cut off from the blasphemers in every place, and those who plan violence and those who commit blasphemy shall perish by the sword.]

[18]And now I tell you, my sons, and show you
The paths of righteousness and the paths of violence.
Yea, I will show them to you again
That ye may know what will come to pass.

[19]And now, hearken unto me, my sons,
And walk in the paths of righteousness,
And walk not in the paths of violence;
For all who walk in the paths of unrighteousness shall perish forever.'

Chapters 92, 91:1-10, 18-19

Enoch's Book of Admonition for his Children

CHAPTER 92

[1]The book written by Enoch -[Enoch indeed wrote this complete doctrine of wisdom, (which is) praised of all men and a judge of all the earth] for all my children who shall dwell on the earth. And for the future generations who shall observe uprightness and peace.

[2]Let not your spirit be troubled on account of the times;
For the Holy and Great One has appointed days for all things.

[3]And the righteous one shall arise from sleep,
[Shall arise] and walk in the paths of righteousness,
And all his path and conversation shall be in eternal goodness and grace.

[4]He will be gracious to the righteous and give him eternal uprightness,
And He will give him power so that he shall be (endowed) with goodness and righteousness.
And he shall walk in eternal light.

[5]And sin shall perish in darkness forever,
And shall no more be seen from that day for evermore.

Chapter 93, 91:12-17

The Apocalypse of Weeks

CHAPTER 93

[1,2]And after that Enoch both gave and began to recount from the books. And Enoch said:

'Concerning the children of righteousness and concerning the elect of the world,
And concerning the plant of uprightness, I will speak these things,
Yea, I Enoch will declare (them) unto you, my sons:

According to that which appeared to me in the heavenly vision,
And which I have known through the word of the holy angels,
And have learnt from the heavenly tablets.'

[3]And Enoch began to recount from the books and said:
'I was born the seventh in the first week,

While judgment and righteousness still endured.

[4]And after me there shall arise in the second week great wickedness,
And deceit shall have sprung up;
And in it there shall be the first end.

And in it a man shall be saved;
And after it is ended unrighteousness shall grow up,
And a law shall be made for the sinners.

[5]And after that in the third week at its close
A man shall be elected as the plant of righteous judgment,
And his posterity shall become the plant of righteousness for evermore.

[6]And after that in the fourth week, at its close,
Visions of the holy and righteous shall be seen,
And a law for all generations and an enclosure shall be made for them.

[7]And after that in the fifth week, at its close,
The house of glory and dominion shall be built for ever.

[8]And after that in the sixth week all who live in it shall be blinded,
And the hearts of all of them shall godlessly forsake wisdom.

And in it a man shall ascend;
And at its close the house of dominion shall be burnt with fire,
And the whole race of the chosen root shall be dispersed.

[9]And after that in the seventh week shall an apostate generation arise,
And many shall be its deeds,
And all its deeds shall be apostate.

[10]And at its close shall be elected
The elect righteous of the eternal plant of righteousness,
To receive sevenfold instruction concerning all His creation.

[11][For who is there of all the children of men that is able to hear the voice of the Holy One without being troubled? And who can think His thoughts? and who is there that can behold all the works [12]of heaven? And how should there be one who could behold the heaven, and who is there that could understand the things of heaven and see a soul or a spirit and could tell thereof, or ascend and see [13]all their ends and think them or do like them? And who is there of all men that could know what is the breadth and the length of the earth, and to whom has been shown the measure of all of them? [14]Or is there anyone who could discern the length of the heaven and how great is its height, and upon what it is founded, and how great is the number of the stars, and where all the luminaries rest?]

Chapter 91:12-17

The Last Three Weeks
(included in some versions only)

CHAPTER 91

[12]And after that there shall be another, the eighth week, that of righteousness,
And a sword shall be given to it that a righteous judgment may be executed on the oppressors,
And sinners shall be delivered into the hands of the righteous.

[13]And at its close they shall acquire houses through their righteousness,
And a house shall be built for the Great King in glory for evermore,

[14d]And all mankind shall look to the path of uprightness.

[14a]And after that, in the ninth week, the righteous judgment shall be revealed to the whole world,

[b]And all the works of the godless shall vanish from all the earth,

[c]And the world shall be written down for destruction.

[15]And after this, in the tenth week in the seventh part,
There shall be the great eternal judgment,
In which He will execute vengeance amongst the angels.

[16]And the first heaven shall depart and pass away,
And a new heaven shall appear,
And all the powers of the heavens shall give sevenfold light.

[17]And after that there will be many weeks without number for ever,
And all shall be in goodness and righteousness,
And sin shall no more be mentioned forever.

Chapter 94:1-5

Admonitions to the Righteous

CHAPTER 94

[1]And now I say unto you, my sons, love righteousness and walk therein;
For the paths of righteousness are worthy of acceptation,
But the paths of unrighteousness shall suddenly be destroyed and vanish.

[2]And to certain men of a generation shall the paths of violence and of death be revealed,
And they shall hold themselves afar from them,
And shall not follow them.

[3]And now I say unto you the righteous:
Walk not in the paths of wickedness, nor in the paths of death,
And draw not nigh to them, lest ye be destroyed.

[4]But seek and choose for yourselves righteousness and an elect life,
And walk in the paths of peace,
And ye shall live and prosper.

[5]And hold fast my words in the thoughts of your hearts,
And suffer them not to be effaced from your hearts;

For I know that sinners will tempt men to evilly-entreat wisdom,
So that no place may be found for her,
And no manner of temptation may minish.

Chapter 94:6-11

Woes for the Sinners

[6]Woe to those who build unrighteousness and oppression
And lay deceit as a foundation;
For they shall be suddenly overthrown,
And they shall have no peace.

[7]Woe to those who build their houses with sin;
For from all their foundations shall they be overthrown,
And by the sword shall they fall.
[And those who acquire gold and silver in judgment suddenly shall perish.]

[8]Woe to you, ye rich, for ye have trusted in your riches,
And from your riches shall ye depart,
Because ye have not remembered the Most High in the days of your riches.

[9]Ye have committed blasphemy and unrighteousness,
And have become ready for the day of slaughter,
And the day of darkness and the day of the great judgment.

[10]Thus I speak and declare unto you:
He who hath created you will overthrow you,
And for your fall there shall be no compassion,
And your Creator will rejoice at your destruction.

[11]And your righteous ones in those days shall be
A reproach to the sinners and the godless.

CHAPTER 95

Enoch's Grief: fresh Woes against the Sinners

[1]Oh that mine eyes were [a cloud of] waters
That I might weep over you,
And pour down my tears as a cloud of waters:
That so I might rest from my trouble of heart!

[2]Who has permitted you to practice reproaches and wickedness?
And so judgment shall overtake you, sinners.

[3]Fear not the sinners, ye righteous;
For again will the Lord deliver them into your hands,
That ye may execute judgment upon them according to your desires.

[4]Woe to you who fulminate anathemas which cannot be reversed:
Healing shall therefore be far from you because of your sins.

[5]Woe to you who requite your neighbor with evil;
For ye shall be requited according to your works.

[6]Woe to you, lying witnesses,
And to those who weigh out injustice,
For suddenly shall ye perish.

[7]Woe to you, sinners, for ye persecute the righteous;
For ye shall be delivered up and persecuted because of injustice,
And heavy shall its yoke be upon you.

CHAPTER 96

Grounds of Hopefulness for the Righteous:
Woes for the Wicked

[1]Be hopeful, ye righteous; for suddenly shall the sinners perish before you,
And ye shall have lordship over them according to your desires.

[2][And in the day of the tribulation of the sinners,
Your children shall mount and rise as eagles,
And higher than the vultures will be your nest,
And ye shall ascend and enter the crevices of the earth,
And the clefts of the rock for ever as coneys before the unrighteous,
And the sirens shall sigh because of you-and weep.]

[3]Wherefore fear not, ye that have suffered;
For healing shall be your portion,
And a bright light shall enlighten you,
And the voice of rest ye shall hear from heaven.

[4]Woe unto you, ye sinners, for your riches make you appear like the righteous,
But your hearts convict you of being sinners,
And this fact shall be a testimony against you for a memorial of (your) evil deeds.

[5]Woe to you who devour the finest of the wheat,
And drink wine in large bowls,
And tread underfoot the lowly with your might.

[6]Woe to you who drink water from every fountain,
For suddenly shall ye be consumed and wither away,
Because ye have forsaken the fountain of life.

[7]Woe to you who work unrighteousness
And deceit and blasphemy:
It shall be a memorial against you for evil.

[8]Woe to you, ye mighty,
Who with might oppress the righteous;
For the day of your destruction is coming.

In those days many and good days shall come to the righteous -in the day of your judgment.

CHAPTER 97

The Evils in Store for Sinners and the Possessors of
Unrighteous Wealth

[1]Believe, ye righteous, that the sinners will become a shame
And perish in the day of unrighteousness.

[2]Be it known unto you (ye sinners) that the Most High is mindful of your destruction,
And the angels of heaven rejoice over your destruction.

[3]What will ye do, ye sinners,
And whither will ye flee on that day of judgment,
When ye hear the voice of the prayer of the righteous?

[4]Yea, ye shall fare like unto them,
Against whom this word shall be a testimony:
"Ye have been companions of sinners."

[5]And in those days the prayer of the righteous shall reach unto the Lord,
And for you the days of your judgment shall come.

[6]And all the words of your unrighteousness shall be read out before the Great Holy One,
And your faces shall be covered with shame,
And He will reject every work which is grounded on unrighteousness.

[7]Woe to you, ye sinners, who live on the mid ocean and on the dry land,
Whose remembrance is evil against you.

[8]Woe to you who acquire silver and gold in unrighteousness and say:
"We have become rich with riches and have possessions;
And have acquired everything we have desired.

[9]And now let us do what we purposed:
For we have gathered silver,

[9c]And many are the husbandmen in our houses."

[9d]And our granaries are (brim) full as with water,

[10]Yea and like water your lies shall flow away;
For your riches shall not abide
But speedily ascend from you;

For ye have acquired it all in unrighteousness,
And ye shall be given over to a great curse.

CHAPTER 98

Self-indulgence of Sinners: Sin originated by Man: all Sin
recorded in Heaven: Woes for the Sinners

[1]And now I swear unto you, to the wise and to the foolish,
For ye shall have manifold experiences on the earth.

[2]For ye men shall put on more adornments than a woman,
And colored garments more than a virgin:
In royalty and in grandeur and in power,
And in silver and in gold and in purple,
And in splendor and in food they shall be poured out as water.

[3]Therefore they shall be wanting in doctrine and wisdom,
And they shall perish thereby together with their possessions;
And with all their glory and their splendor,
And in shame and in slaughter and in great destitution,
Their spirits shall be cast into the furnace of fire.

[4]I have sworn unto you, ye sinners, as a mountain has not become a slave,
And a hill does not become the handmaid of a woman,
Even so sin has not been sent upon the earth,
But man of himself has created it,
And under a great curse shall they fall who commit it.

[5]And barrenness has not been given to the woman,
But on account of the deeds of her own hands she dies without children.

[6]I have sworn unto you, ye sinners, by the Holy Great One,
That all your evil deeds are revealed in the heavens,
And that none of your deeds of oppression are covered and hidden.

[7]And do not think in your spirit nor say in your heart that ye do not know and that ye do not see [8]that every sin is every day recorded in heaven in the presence of the Most High. From henceforth ye know that all your oppression wherewith ye oppress is written down every day till the day of your judgment. [9]Woe to you, ye fools, for through your folly shall ye perish: and ye transgress against the wise, [10]and so good hap shall not be your portion. And now, know ye that ye are prepared for the day of

destruction: wherefore do not hope to live, ye sinners, but ye shall depart and die; for ye know no ransom; for ye are prepared for the day of the great judgment, for the day of tribulation and great shame for your spirits. [11]Woe to you, ye obstinate of heart, who work wickedness and eat blood: Whence have ye good things to eat and to drink and to be filled? From all the good things which the Lord the Most High has placed in abundance on the earth; therefore ye shall have no peace. [12]Woe to you who love the deeds of unrighteousness: wherefore do ye hope for good hap unto yourselves? know that ye shall be delivered into the hands of the righteous, and they shall cut [13]off your necks and slay you, and have no mercy upon you. Woe to you who rejoice in the tribulation [14]of the righteous; for no grave shall be dug for you. Woe to you who set at nought the words of [15]the righteous; for ye shall have no hope of life. Woe to you who write down lying and godless words; for they write down their lies that men may hear them and act godlessly towards (their) [16]neighbor. Therefore they shall have no peace but die a sudden death.

CHAPTER 99

*Woes pronounced on the Godless, the Lawbreakers: evil
Plight of Sinners in The Last Days: further Woes*

[1]Woe to you who work godlessness,
And glory in lying and extol them:
Ye shall perish, and no happy life shall be yours.

[2]Woe to them who pervert the words of uprightness,
And transgress the eternal law,
And transform themselves into what they were not [into sinners]:
They shall be trodden under foot upon the earth.

[3]In those days make ready, ye righteous, to raise your prayers as a memorial,
And place them as a testimony before the angels,
That they may place the sin of the sinners for a memorial before the Most High.

[4]In those days the nations shall be stirred up,
And the families of the nations shall arise on the day of destruction.

[5]And in those days the destitute shall go forth and carry off their children,
And they shall abandon them, so that their children shall perish through them:
Yea, they shall abandon their children (that are still) sucklings, and not return to them,
And shall have no pity on their beloved ones.

^{6,7}And again I swear to you, ye sinners, that sin is prepared for a day of unceasing bloodshed. And they who worship stones, and grave images of gold and silver and wood (and stone) and clay, and those who worship impure spirits and demons, and all kinds of idols not according to knowledge, shall get no manner of help from them.

⁸And they shall become godless by reason of the folly of their hearts,
And their eyes shall be blinded through the fear of their hearts
And through visions in their dreams.

⁹Through these they shall become godless and fearful;
For they shall have wrought all their work in a lie,
And shall have worshiped a stone:
Therefore in an instant shall they perish.

¹⁰But in those days blessed are all they who accept the words of wisdom, and understand them,
And observe the paths of the Most High, and walk in the path of His righteousness,
And become not godless with the godless;
For they shall be saved.

¹¹Woe to you who spread evil to your neighbors;
For you shall be slain in Sheol.

¹²Woe to you who make deceitful and false measures,
And (to them) who cause bitterness on the earth;
For they shall thereby be utterly consumed.

¹³Woe to you who build your houses through the grievous toil of others,
And all their building materials are the bricks and stones of sin;
I tell you ye shall have no peace.

¹⁴Woe to them who reject the measure and eternal heritage of their fathers
And whose souls follow after idols;
For they shall have no rest.

¹⁵Woe to them who work unrighteousness and help oppression,
And slay their neighbors until the day of the great judgment.

¹⁶For He shall cast down your glory,
And bring affliction on your hearts,
And shall arouse His fierce indignation
And destroy you all with the sword;
And all the holy and righteous shall remember your sins.

CHAPTER 100

The Sinners destroy each other: Judgment of the Fallen Angels: the Safety of
the Righteous: further Woes for the Sinners

¹And in those days in one place the fathers together with their sons shall be smitten
And brothers one with another shall fall in death
Till the streams flow with their blood.

²For a man shall not withhold his hand from slaying his sons and his sons' sons,
And the sinner shall not withhold his hand from his honored brother:
From dawn till sunset they shall slay one another.

³And the horse shall walk up to the breast in the blood of sinners,
And the chariot shall be submerged to its height.

⁴In those days the angels shall descend into the secret places
And gather together into one place all those who brought down sin
And the Most High will arise on that day of judgment
To execute great judgment amongst sinners.

⁵And over all the righteous and holy He will appoint guardians from amongst the holy angels
To guard them as the apple of an eye,
Until He makes an end of all wickedness and all sin,
And though the righteous sleep a long sleep, they have nought to fear.

⁶And (then) the children of the earth shall see the wise in security,
And shall understand all the words of this book,
And recognize that their riches shall not be able to save them
In the overthrow of their sins.

⁷Woe to you, Sinners, on the day of strong anguish,
Ye who afflict the righteous and burn them with fire:
Ye shall be requited according to your works.

⁸Woe to you, ye obstinate of heart,
Who watch in order to devise wickedness:
Therefore shall fear come upon you
And there shall be none to help you.

⁹Woe to you, ye sinners, on account of the words of your mouth,
And on account of the deeds of your hands which your godlessness as wrought,

In blazing flames burning worse than fire shall ye burn.

[10]And now, know ye that from the angels He will inquire as to your deeds in heaven, from the sun and from the moon and from the stars in reference to your sins because upon the earth ye execute [11]judgment on the righteous. And He will summon to testify against you every cloud and mist and dew and rain; for they shall all be withheld because of you from descending upon you, and they [12]shall be mindful of your sins. And now give presents to the rain that it be not withheld from descending upon you, nor yet the dew, when it has received gold and silver from you that it may descend. [13]When the hoarfrost and snow with their chilliness, and all the snowstorms with all their plagues fall upon you, in those days ye shall not be able to stand before them.

CHAPTER 101

Exhortation to the fear of God: all Nature
fears Him but not the Sinners

[1]Observe the heaven, ye children of heaven, and every work of the Most High, and fear ye Him [2]and work no evil in His presence. If He closes the windows of heaven, and withholds the rain and [3]the dew from descending on the earth on your account, what will ye do then? And if He sends His anger upon you because of your deeds, ye cannot petition Him; for ye spake proud and insolent [4]words against His righteousness: therefore ye shall have no peace. And see ye not the sailors of the ships, how their ships are tossed to and fro by the waves, and are shaken by the winds, and are [5]in sore trouble? And therefore do they fear because all their goodly possessions go upon the sea with them, and they have evil forebodings of heart that the sea will swallow them and they will [6]perish therein. Are not the entire sea and all its waters, and all its movements, the work of the Most [7]High, and has He not set limits to its doings, and confined it throughout by the sand? And at His reproof it is afraid and dries up, and all its fish die and all that is in it; But ye sinners that are [8]on the earth fear Him not. Has He not made the heaven and the earth, and all that is therein? Who has given understanding and wisdom to everything that moves on the earth and in the sea. [9]Do not the sailors of the ships fear the sea? Yet sinners fear not the Most High.

CHAPTER 102

Terrors of the Day of Judgment: the adverse Fortunes of the
Righteous on the Earth

[1]In those days when He hath brought a grievous fire upon you,
Whither will ye flee, and where will ye find deliverance?
And when He launches forth His Word against you Will you not be affrighted
and fear?

[2]And all the luminaries shall be affrighted with great fear,
And all the earth shall be affrighted and tremble and be alarmed.

[3]And all the angels shall execute their commands
And shall seek to hide themselves from the presence of the Great Glory,
And the children of earth shall tremble and quake;
And ye sinners shall be cursed forever,
And ye shall have no peace.

[4]Fear ye not, ye souls of the righteous,
And be hopeful ye that have died in righteousness.

[5]And grieve not if your soul into Sheol has descended in grief,
And that in your life your body fared not according to your goodness,
But wait for the day of the judgment of sinners
And for the day of cursing and chastisement.

[6]And yet when ye die the sinners speak over you:
"As we die, so die the righteous,
And what benefit do they reap for their deeds?

[7]Behold, even as we, so do they die in grief and darkness,
And what have they more than we?
From henceforth we are equal.

[8]And what will they receive and what will they see forever?
Behold, they too have died,
And henceforth for ever shall they see no light."

[9]I tell you, ye sinners, ye are content to eat and drink, and rob and sin, and strip men naked, and [10]acquire wealth and see good days. Have ye seen the righteous how their end falls out, that no manner [11]of violence is found in them till their death? "Nevertheless they perished and became as though they had not been, and their spirits descended into Sheol in tribulation."

CHAPTER 103

Different Destinies of the Righteous and the Sinners: fresh
Objections of the Sinners

[1]Now, therefore, I swear to you, the righteous, by the glory of the Great and Honored and [2]Mighty One in dominion, and by His greatness I swear to you.

I know a mystery
And have read the heavenly tablets,
And have seen the holy books,
And have found written therein and inscribed regarding them:

[3]That all goodness and joy and glory are prepared for them,
And written down for the spirits of those who have died in righteousness,
And that manifold good shall be given to you in recompense for your labors,
And that your lot is abundantly beyond the lot of the living.

[4]And the spirits of you who have died in righteousness shall live and rejoice,
And their spirits shall not perish, nor their memorial from before the face of the Great One
Unto all the generations of the world: wherefore no longer fear their contumely.

[5]Woe to you, ye sinners, when ye have died,
If ye die in the wealth of your sins,
And those who are like you say regarding you:
"Blessed are the sinners: they have seen all their days.

[6]And how they have died in prosperity and in wealth,
And have not seen tribulation or murder in their life;
And they have died in honor,
And judgment has not been executed on them during their life."

[7]Know ye, that their souls will be made to descend into Sheol
And they shall be wretched in their great tribulation.

[8]And into darkness and chains and a burning flame where there is grievous judgment shall your spirits enter;
And the great judgment shall be for all the generations of the world.
Woe to you, for ye shall have no peace.

[9]Say not in regard to the righteous and good who are in life:
"In our troubled days we have toiled laboriously and experienced every trouble,
And met with much evil and been consumed,

And have become few and our spirit small.

¹⁰And we have been destroyed and have not found any to help us even with a word:

We have been tortured [and destroyed], and not hoped to see life from day to day.

¹¹We hoped to be the head and have become the tail:

We have toiled laboriously and had no satisfaction in our toil;

And we have become the food of the sinners and the unrighteous,

And they have laid their yoke heavily upon us.

¹²They have had dominion over us that hated us and smote us;

And to those that hated us we have bowed our necks

But they pitied us not.

¹³We desired to get away from them that we might escape and be at rest,

But found no place whereunto we should flee and be safe from them.

¹⁴And are complained to the rulers in our tribulation,

And cried out against those who devoured us,

But they did not attend to our cries

And would not hearken to our voice.

¹⁵And they helped those who robbed us and devoured us and those who made us few; and they concealed their oppression, and they did not remove from us the yoke of those that devoured us and dispersed us and murdered us, and they concealed their murder, and remembered not that they had lifted up their hands against us.

CHAPTER 104

Assurances given to the Righteous: Admonitions to Sinners
and the Falsifiers of the Words of Uprightness

¹I swear unto you, that in heaven the angels remember you for good before the glory of the Great ²One: and your names are written before the glory of the Great One. Be hopeful; for aforetime ye were put to shame through ill and affliction; but now ye shall shine as the lights of heaven, ³ye shall shine and ye shall be seen, and the portals of heaven shall be opened to you. And in your cry, cry for judgment, and it shall appear to you; for all your tribulation shall be visited on the ⁴rulers, and on all who helped those who plundered you. Be hopeful, and cast not away your hope; ⁵for ye shall have great joy as the angels of heaven. What shall ye be obliged to do? Ye shall not have to hide on

the day of the great judgment and ye shall not be found as sinners, and the eternal [6]judgment shall be far from you for all the generations of the world. And now fear not, ye righteous, when ye see the sinners growing strong and prospering in their ways: be not companions with them, [7]but keep afar from their violence; for ye shall become companions of the hosts of heaven. And, although ye sinners say: "All our sins shall not be searched out and be written down," nevertheless [8]they shall write down all your sins every day. And now I show unto you that light and darkness, [9]day and night, see all your sins. Be not godless in your hearts, and lie not and alter not the words of uprightness, nor charge with lying the words of the Holy Great One, nor take account of your [10]idols; for all your lying and all your godlessness issue not in righteousness but in great sin. And now I know this mystery, that sinners will alter and pervert the words of righteousness in many ways, and will speak wicked words, and lie, and practice great deceits, and write books concerning [11]their words. But when they write down truthfully all my words in their languages, and do not change or minish ought from my words but write them all down truthfully -all that I first testified [12]concerning them. Then, I know another mystery, that books will be given to the righteous and the [13]wise to become a cause of joy and uprightness and much wisdom. And to them shall the books be given, and they shall believe in them and rejoice over them, and then shall all the righteous who have learnt therefrom all the paths of uprightness be recompensed.'

CHAPTER 105

God and the Messiah to dwell with Man

[1]In those days the Lord bade (them) to summon and testify to the children of earth concerning their wisdom: Show (it) unto them; for ye are their guides, and a recompense over the whole earth. [2]For I and My son will be united with them forever in the paths of uprightness in their lives; and ye shall have peace: rejoice, ye children of uprightness. Amen.

CHAPTER 106

Fragment of the Book of Noah

[1]And after some days my son Methuselah took a wife for his son Lamech, and she became [2]pregnant by him and bore a son. And his body was white as snow and red as the blooming of a rose, and the hair of his head and his long locks were white as wool,

and his eyes beautiful. And when he opencd his eyes, he lighted up the whole house like the sun, and the whole house [3]was very bright. And thereupon he arose in the hands of the midwife, opened his mouth, and conversed with the Lord of righteousness. [4]And his father Lamech was afraid of him and [5]fled, and came to his father Methuselah. And he said unto him: 'I have begotten a strange son, diverse from and unlike man, and resembling the sons of the God of heaven; and his nature is different and he is not like us, and his eyes are as the rays of the sun, and his [6]countenance is glorious. And it seems to me that he is not sprung from me but from the angels, and I fear that in his days a wonder may be [7]wrought on the earth. And now, my father, I am here to petition thee and implore thee that thou mayest go to Enoch, our father, and learn from him the truth, for his dwelling-place is [8]amongst the angels.' And when Methuselah heard the words of his son, he came to me to the ends of the earth; for he had heard that I was there, and he cried aloud, and I heard his voice and I came to him. And I said unto him: 'Behold, here am I, my son, wherefore hast [9]thou come to me?' And he answered and said: 'Because of a great cause of anxiety have I come to thee, and because of a disturbing vision [10]have I approached. And now, my father, hear me: unto Lamech my son there hath been born a son, the like of whom there is none, and his nature is not like man's nature, and the color of his body is whiter than snow and redder than the bloom of a rose, and the hair of his head is whiter than white wool, and his eyes are like the rays of the sun, and he opened his eyes and [11]thereupon lighted up the whole house. And he arose in the hands of the midwife, and opened [12]his mouth and blessed the Lord of heaven. And his father Lamech became afraid and fled to me, and did not believe that he was sprung from him, but that he was in the likeness of the angels of heaven; and behold I have come to thee that thou mayest make known to me the truth.' [13]And I, Enoch, answered and said unto him: 'The Lord will do a new thing on the earth, and this I have already seen in a vision, and make known to thee that in the generation of my father Jared some of the angels of heaven [14]transgressed the word of the Lord. And behold they commit sin and transgress the law, and have united themselves with women and commit sin with them, and have married some of them, [17]and have begot children by them. And they shall produce on the earth giants not according to the spirit, but according to the flesh, and there shall be a great punishment on the earth, and the [15]earth shall be cleansed from all impurity. Yea, there shall come a great destruction over the whole earth, and there shall be a deluge and [16]a great destruction for one year. And this son who has been born unto you shall be left on the earth, and his three children shall be saved with him: when all mankind that are on the earth [18]shall die [he and his sons shall be saved]. And now make known to thy son Lamech that he who has been born is in truth his son, and call his name Noah; for he shall be left to you, and he and his sons shall be saved from the destruction, which shall come upon the earth on account of all the sin and all the unrighteousness, which shall be consummated on the earth in his days. [19]And after that there shall be still more unrighteousness than that which was first consummated on the earth; for I know the mysteries of the holy ones; for He, the Lord, has showed me and informed me, and I have read (them) in the heavenly tablets.

CHAPTER 107

[1]And I saw written on them that generation upon generation shall transgress, till a generation of righteousness arises, and transgression is destroyed and sin passes away from the earth, and all [2]manner of good comes upon it. And now, my son, go and make known to thy son Lamech that this [3]son, which has been born, is in truth his son, and that (this) is no lie.' And when Methuselah had heard the words of his father Enoch – for he had shown to him everything in secret– he returned and showed (them) to him and called the name of that son Noah; for he will comfort the earth after all the destruction.

CHAPTER 108

[1]Another book which Enoch wrote for his son Methuselah and for those who will come after him, [2]and keep the law in the last days. Ye who have done good shall wait for those days till an end is [3]made of those who work evil; and an end of the might of the transgressors. And wait ye indeed till sin has passed away, for their names shall be blotted out of the book of life and out of the holy books, and their seed shall be destroyed forever, and their spirits shall be slain, and they shall cry and make lamentation in a place that is a chaotic wilderness, and in the fire shall they [4]burn; for there is no earth there. And I saw there something like an invisible cloud; for by reason of its depth I could not look over, and I saw a flame of fire blazing brightly, and things like shining [5]mountains circling and sweeping to and fro. And I asked one of the holy angels who was with me and said unto him: 'What is this shining thing? for it is not a heaven but only the flame of a blazing [6]fire, and the voice of weeping and crying and lamentation and strong pain.' And he said unto me: 'This place which thou seest-here are cast the spirits of sinners and blasphemers, and of those who work wickedness, and of those who pervert everything that the Lord hath spoken through the mouth [7]of the prophets -(even) the things that shall be. For some of them are written and inscribed above in the heaven, in order that the angels may read them and know that which shall befall the sinners, and the spirits of the humble, and of those who have afflicted their bodies, and been recompensed [8]by God; and of those who have been put to shame by

wicked men: Who love God and loved neither gold nor silver nor any of the good things which are in the world, but gave over their bodies to [9]torture. Who, since they came into being, longed not after earthly food, but regarded everything as a passing breath, and lived accordingly, and the Lord tried them much, and their spirits were [10]found pure so that they should bless His name. And all the blessings destined for them I have recounted in the books. And he hath assigned them their recompense, because they have been found to be such as loved heaven more than their life in the world, and though they were trodden under foot of wicked men, and experienced abuse and reviling from them and were put to shame, [11]yet they blessed Me. And now I will summon the spirits of the good who belong to the generation of light, and I will transform those who were born in darkness, who in the flesh were not recompensed [12]with such honor as their faithfulness deserved. And I will bring forth in shining light those who [13]have loved My holy name, and I will seat each on the throne of his honor. And they shall be resplendent for times without number; for righteousness is the judgment of God; for to the faithful [14]He will give faithfulness in the habitation of upright paths. And they shall see those who were [15]born in darkness led into darkness, while the righteous shall be resplendent. And the sinners shall cry aloud and see them resplendent, and they indeed will go where days and seasons are prescribed for them.

The Book of the Secrets of Enoch

Chapter 1

[1]There was a wise man, a great artificer, and the Lord conceived love for him and received him, that he should behold the uppermost dwellings and be an eyewitness of the wise and great and inconceivable and immutable realm of God Almighty, of the very wonderful and glorious and bright and many-eyed station of the Lord's servants, and of the inaccessible throne of the Lord, and of the degrees and manifestations of the incorporeal hosts, and of the ineffable ministration of the multitude of the elements, and of the various apparition and inexpressible singing of the host of Cherubim, and of the boundless light.

[2]At that time, he said, when my one hundred and sixty-fifth year was completed, I begat my son Mathusal (Methuselah).

[3]After this too I lived two hundred years and completed of all the years of my life three hundred and sixty-five years.

[4]On the first day of the month I was in my house alone and was resting on my bed and slept.

[5]And when I was asleep, great distress came up into my heart, and I was weeping with my eyes in sleep, and I could not understand what this distress was, or what would happen to me.

[6]And there appeared to me two men, exceeding big, so that I never saw such on earth; their faces were shining like the sun, their eyes too (were) like a burning light, and from their lips was fire coming forth with clothing and singing of various kinds in appearance purple, their wings (were)brighter than gold, their hands whiter than snow.

[7]They were standing at the head of my bed and began to call me by my name.

[8]And I arose from my sleep and saw clearly those two men standing in front of me.

[9]And I saluted them and was seized with fear and the appearance of my face was changed from terror, and those men said to me:

[10]Have courage, Enoch, do not fear; the eternal God sent us to you, and lo! You shalt today ascend with us into heaven, and you shall tell your sons and all your household all that they shall do without you on earth in your house, and let no one seek you till the Lord return you to them.

[11]And I made haste to obey them and went out from my house, and made to the doors, as it was ordered me, and summoned my sons Mathusal (Methuselah) and Regim and Gaidad and made known to them all the marvels those (men) had told me.

Chapter 2

[1]Listen to me, my children, I know not whither I go, or what will befall me; now therefore, my children, I tell you: turn not from God before the face of the vain, who made not Heaven and earth, for these shall perish and those who worship them, and may the Lord make confident your hearts in the fear of him. And now, my children, let no one think to seek me, until the Lord return me to you.

Chapter 3

[1]It came to pass, when Enoch had told his sons, that the angels took him on to their wings and bore him up on to the first heaven and placed him on the clouds. And there I looked, and again I looked higher, and saw the ether, and they placed me on the first heaven and showed me a very great Sea, greater than the earthly sea.

Chapter 4

[1]They brought before my face the elders and rulers of the stellar orders, and showed me two hundred angels, who rule the stars and (their) services to the heavens, and fly with their wings and come round all those who sail.

Chapter 5

[1]And here I looked down and saw the treasure-houses of the snow, and the angels who keep their terrible storehouses, and the clouds whence they come out and into which they go.

Chapter 6

¹They showed me the treasure-house of the dew, like oil of the olive, and the appearance of its form, as of all the flowers of the earth; further many angels guarding the treasure-houses of these (things), and how they are made to shut and open.

Chapter 7

¹And those men took me and led me up on to the second heaven, and showed me darkness, greater than earthly darkness, and there I saw prisoners hanging, watched, awaiting the great and boundless judgment, and these angels (spirits) were dark-looking, more than earthly darkness, and incessantly making weeping through all hours.

²And I said to the men who were with me: Wherefore are these incessantly tortured? They answered me: These are God's apostates, who obeyed not God's commands, but took counsel with their own will, and turned away with their prince, who also (is) fastened on the fifth heaven.

³And I felt great pity for them, and they saluted me, and said to me: Man of God, pray for us to the Lord; and I answered to them: Who am I, a mortal man, that I should pray for angels (spirits)? Who knows whither I go, or what will befall me? Or who will pray for me?

Chapter 8

¹And those men took me thence, and led me up on to the third heaven, and placed me there; and I looked downwards, and saw the produce of these places, such as has never been known for goodness.

²And I saw all the sweet-flowering trees and beheld their fruits, which were sweet-smelling, and all the foods borne (by them) bubbling with fragrant exhalation.

³And in the midst of the trees that of life, in that place whereon the Lord rests, when he goes up into paradise; and this tree is of ineffable goodness and fragrance, and adorned more than every existing thing; and on all sides (it is) in form gold-looking and vermilion and fire-like and covers all, and it has produce from all fruits.

[4]Its root is in the garden at the earth's end.

[5]And paradise is between corruptibility and incorruptibility.

[6]And two springs come out which send forth honey and milk, and their springs send forth oil and wine, and they separate into four parts, and go round with quiet course, and go down into the PARADISE OF EDEN, between corruptibility and incorruptibility.

[7]And thence they go forth along the earth, and have a revolution to their circle even as other elements.

[8]And here there is no unfruitful tree, and every place is blessed.

[9]And (there are) three hundred angels very bright, who keep the garden, and with incessant sweet singing and never-silent voices serve the Lord throughout all days and hours.

[10]And I said: How very sweet is this place, and those men said to me:

Chapter 9

[1]This place, O Enoch, is prepared for the righteous, who endure all manner of offence from those that exasperate their souls, who avert their eyes from iniquity, and make righteous judgment, and give bread to the hungering, and cover the naked with clothing, and raise up the fallen, and help injured orphans, and who walk without fault before the face of the Lord, and serve him alone, and for them is prepared this place for eternal inheritance.

Chapter 10

[1]And those two men led me up on to the Northern side, and showed me there a very terrible place, and (there were) all manner of tortures in that place: cruel darkness and unillumined gloom, and there is no light there, but murky fire constantly flaming aloft, and (there is) a fiery river coming forth, and that whole place is everywhere fire, and everywhere (there is) frost and ice, thirst and shivering, while the bonds are very cruel, and the angels (spirits) fearful and merciless, bearing angry weapons, merciless torture, and I said:

[2]Woe, woe, how very terrible is this place.

[3]And those men said to me: This place, O Enoch, is prepared for those who dishonor God, who on earth practice sin against nature, which is child-corruption after the sodomitic fashion, magic-making, enchantments and devilish witchcrafts, and who boast of their wicked deeds, stealing, lies, calumnies, envy, rancor, fornication, murder, and who, accursed, steal the souls of men, who, seeing the poor take away their goods and themselves wax rich, injuring them for other men's goods; who being able to satisfy the empty, made the hungering to die; being able to clothe, stripped the naked; and who knew not their creator, and bowed to the soulless (and lifeless) gods, who cannot see nor hear, vain gods, (who also) built hewn images and bow down to unclean handiwork, for all these is prepared this place among these, for eternal inheritance.

Chapter 11

[1]Those men took me, and led me up on to the fourth heaven, and showed me all the successive goings, and all the rays of the light of sun and moon.

[2]And I measure their goings, and compared their light, and saw that the sun's light is greater than the moon's.

[3]Its circle and the wheels on which it goes always, like the wind going past with very marvelous speed, and day and night it has no rest.

[4]Its passage and return (are accompanied by) four great stars, (and) each star has under it a thousand stars, to the right of the sun's wheel, (and by) four to the left, each having under it a thousand stars, altogether eight thousand, issuing with the sun continually.

[5]And by day fifteen myriads of angels attend it, and by night A thousand.

[6]And six-winged ones issue with the angels before the sun's wheel into the fiery flames, and a hundred angels kindle the sun and set it alight.

Chapter 12

[1]And I looked and saw other flying elements of the sun, whose names (are) Phoenixes and Chalkydri, marvelous and wonderful, with feet and tails in the form of a lion, and a crocodile's head, their appearance (is) empurpled, like the rainbow; their size (is) nine hundred measures, their wings (are like) those of angels, each (has) twelve, and they attend and accompany the sun, bearing heat and dew, as it is ordered them from God.

[2]Thus (the sun) revolves and goes, and rises under the heaven, and its course goes under the earth with the light of its rays incessantly.

Chapter 13

[1]Those men bore me away to the east, and placed me at the sun's gates, where the sun goes forth according to the regulation of the seasons and the circuit of the months of the whole year, and the number of the hours day and night.

[2]And I saw six gates open, each gate having sixty-one stadia and A quarter of one stadium, and I measured (them) truly, and understood their size (to be) so much, through which the sun goes forth, and goes to the west, and is made even, and rises throughout all the months, and turns back again from the six gates according to the succession of the seasons; thus (the period) of the whole year is finished after the returns of the four seasons.

Chapter 14

[1]And again those men led me away to the western parts, and showed me six great gates open corresponding to the eastern gates, opposite to where the sun sets, according to the number of the days three hundred and sixty-five and A quarter.

[2]Thus again it goes down to the western gates, (and) draws away its light, the greatness of its brightness, under the earth; for since the crown of its shining is in heaven with the Lord, and guarded by four hundred angels, while the sun goes round on wheel under the earth, and stands seven great hours in night, and spends half (its course) under the earth, when it comes to the eastern approach in the eighth hour of the night, it brings its lights, and the crown of shining, and the sun flames forth more than fire.

Chapter 15

[1]Then the elements of the sun, called Phoenixes and Chalkydri break into song, therefore every bird flutters with its wings, rejoicing at the giver of light, and they broke into song at the command of the Lord.

^{2}The giver of light comes to give brightness to the whole world, and the morning guard takes shape, which is the rays of the sun, and the sun of the earth goes out, and receives its brightness to light up the whole face of the earth, and they showed me this calculation of the sun's going.

^{3}And the gates which it enters, these are the great gates of the calculation of the hours of the year; for this reason the sun is a great creation, whose circuit (lasts) twenty-eight years, and begins again from the beginning.

Chapter 16

^{1}Those men showed me the other course, that of the moon, twelve great gates, crowned from west to east, by which the moon goes in and out of the customary times.

^{2}It goes in at the first gate to the western places of the sun, by the first gates with (thirty)-one (days) exactly, by the second gates with thirty-one days exactly, by the third with thirty days exactly, by the fourth with thirty days exactly, by the fifth with thirty-one days exactly, by the sixth with thirty-one days exactly, by the seventh with thirty days exactly, by the eighth with thirty-one days perfectly, by the ninth with thirty-one days exactly, by the tenth with thirty days perfectly, by the eleventh with thirty-one days exactly, by the twelfth with twenty-eight days exactly.

^{3}And it goes through the western gates in the order and number of the eastern, and accomplishes the three hundred and sixty-five and a quarter days of the solar year, while the lunar year has three hundred fifty-four, and there are wanting (to it) twelve days of the solar circle, which are the lunar epacts of the whole year.

^{4}Thus, too, the great circle contains five hundred and thirty-two years.

^{5}The quarter (of a day) is omitted for three years, the fourth fulfils it exactly.

^{6}Therefore they are taken outside of heaven for three years and are not added to the number of days, because they change the time of the years to two new months towards completion, to two others towards diminution.

^{7}And when the western gates are finished, it returns and goes to the eastern to the lights, and goes thus day and night about the heavenly circles, lower than all circles, swifter than the heavenly winds, and spirits and elements and angels flying; each angel has six wings.

^{8}It has a sevenfold course in nineteen years.

Chapter 17

[1]In the midst of the heavens I saw armed soldiers, serving the Lord, with tympana and organs, with incessant voice, with sweet voice, with sweet and incessant (voice) and various singing, which it is impossible to describe, and (which) astonishes every mind, so wonderful and marvelous is the singing of those angels, and I was delighted listening to it.

Chapter 18

[1]The men took me on to the fifth heaven and placed me, and there I saw many and countless soldiers, called Grigori, of human appearance, and their size (was) greater than that of great giants and their faces withered, and the silence of their mouths perpetual, and their was no service on the fifth heaven, and I said to the men who were with me:

[2]Wherefore are these very withered and their faces melancholy, and their mouths silent, and (wherefore) is there no service on this heaven?

[3]And they said to me: These are the Grigori, who with their prince Satanail (Satan) rejected the Lord of light, and after them are those who are held in great darkness on the second heaven, and three of them went down on to earth from the Lord's throne, to the place Ermon, and broke through their vows on the shoulder of the hill Ermon and saw the daughters of men how good they are, and took to themselves wives, and befouled the earth with their deeds, who in all times of their age made lawlessness and mixing, and giants are born and marvelous big men and great enmity.

[4]And therefore God judged them with great judgment, and they weep for their brethren and they will be punished on the Lord's great day.

[5]And I said to the Grigori: I saw your brethren and their works, and their great torments, and I prayed for them, but the Lord has condemned them (to be) under earth till (the existing) heaven and earth shall end forever.

[6]And I said: Wherefore do you wait, brethren, and do not serve before the Lord's face, and have not put your services before the Lord's face, lest you anger your Lord utterly?

[7]And they listened to my admonition, and spoke to the four ranks in heaven, and lo! As I stood with those two men four trumpets trumpeted together with great voice, and the Grigori broke into song with one voice, and their voice went up before the Lord pitifully and affectingly.

Chapter 19

[1]And thence those men took me and bore me up on to the sixth heaven, and there I saw seven bands of angels, very bright and very glorious, and their faces shining more than the sun's shining, glistening, and there is no difference in their faces, or behavior, or manner of dress; and these make the orders, and learn the goings of the stars, and the alteration of the moon, or revolution of the sun, and the good government of the world.

[2]And when they see evildoing they make commandments and instruction, and sweet and loud singing, and all (songs) of praise.

[3]These are the archangels who are above angels, measure all life in heaven and on earth, and the angels who are (appointed) over seasons and years, the angels who are over rivers and sea, and who are over the fruits of the earth, and the angels who are over every grass, giving food to all, to every living thing, and the angels who write all the souls of men, and all their deeds, and their lives before the Lord's face; in their midst are six Phoenixes and six Cherubim and six six-winged ones continually with one voice singing one voice, and it is not possible to describe their singing, and they rejoice before the Lord at his footstool.

Chapter 20

[1]And those two men lifted me up thence on to the seventh heaven, and I saw there a very great light, and fiery troops of great archangels, incorporeal forces, and dominions, orders and governments, Cherubim and seraphim, thrones and many-eyed ones, nine regiments, the Ioanit stations of light, and I became afraid, and began to tremble with great terror, and those men took me, and led me after them, and said to me:

[2]Have courage, Enoch, do not fear, and showed me the Lord from afar, sitting on His very high throne. For what is there on the tenth heaven, since the Lord dwells there?

[3]On the tenth heaven is God, in the Hebrew tongue he is called Aravat.

[4]And all the heavenly troops would come and stand on the ten steps according to their rank, and would bow down to the Lord, and would again go to their places in joy and felicity, singing songs in the boundless light with small and tender voices, gloriously serving him.

Chapter 21

[1]And the Cherubim and seraphim standing about the throne, the six-winged and many-eyed ones do not depart, standing before the Lord's face doing his will, and cover his whole throne, singing with gentle voice before the Lord's face: Holy, holy, holy, Lord Ruler of Sabaoth, heavens and earth are full of Your glory.

[2]When I saw all these things, those men said to me: Enoch, thus far is it commanded us to journey with you, and those men went away from me and thereupon I saw them not.

[3]And I remained alone at the end of the seventh heaven and became afraid, and fell on my face and said to myself: Woe is me, what has befallen me?

[4]And the Lord sent one of his glorious ones, the archangel Gabriel, and (he) said to me: Have courage, Enoch, do not fear, arise before the Lord's face into eternity, arise, come with me.

[5]And I answered him, and said in myself: My Lord, my soul is departed from me, from terror and trembling, and I called to the men who led me up to this place, on them I relied, and (it is) with them I go before the Lord's face.

[6]And Gabriel caught me up, as a leaf caught up by the wind, and placed me before the Lord's face.

[7]And I saw the eighth heaven, which is called in the Hebrew tongue Muzaloth, changer of the seasons, of drought, and of wet, and of the twelve constellations of the circle of the firmament, which are above the seventh heaven.

[8]And I saw the ninth heaven, which is called in Hebrew Kuchavim, where are the heavenly homes of the twelve constellations of the circle of the firmament.

Chapter 22

[1]On the tenth heaven, (which is called) Aravoth, I saw the appearance of the Lord's face, like iron made to glow in fire, and brought out, emitting sparks, and it burns.

[2]Thus (in a moment of eternity) I saw the Lord's face, but the Lord's face is ineffable, marvelous and very awful, and very, very terrible.

[3]And who am I to tell of the Lord's unspeakable being, and of his very wonderful face? And I cannot tell the quantity of his many instructions, and various voices, the Lord's throne (is) very great and not made with hands, nor the quantity of those standing

round him, troops of Cherubim and seraphim, nor their incessant singing, nor his immutable beauty, and who shall tell of the ineffable greatness of his glory.

⁴And I fell prone and bowed down to the Lord, and the Lord with his lips said to me:

⁵Have courage, Enoch, do not fear, arise and stand before my face into eternity.

⁶And the archistratege Michael lifted me up, and led me to before the Lord's face.

⁷And the Lord said to his servants tempting them: Let Enoch stand before my face into eternity, and the glorious ones bowed down to the Lord, and said: Let Enoch go according to Your word.

⁸And the Lord said to Michael: Go and take Enoch from out (of) his earthly garments, and anoint him with my sweet ointment, and put him into the garments of My glory.

⁹And Michael did thus, as the Lord told him. He anointed me, and dressed me, and the appearance of that ointment is more than the great light, and his ointment is like sweet dew, and its smell mild, shining like the sun's ray, and I looked at myself, and (I) was like (transfigured) one of his glorious ones.

¹⁰And the Lord summoned one of his archangels by name Pravuil, whose knowledge was quicker in wisdom than the other archangels, who wrote all the deeds of the Lord; and the Lord said to Pravuil: Bring out the books from my storehouses, and a reed of quick-writing, and give (it) to Enoch, and deliver to him the choice and comforting books out of your hand.

Chapter 23

¹And he was telling me all the works of heaven, earth and sea, and all the elements, their passages and goings, and the thunderings of the thunders, the sun and moon, the goings and changes of the stars, the seasons, years, days, and hours, the risings of the wind, the numbers of the angels, and the formation of their songs, and all human things, the tongue of every human song and life, the commandments, instructions, and sweet-voiced singings, and all things that it is fitting to learn.

²And Pravuil told me: All the things that I have told you, we have written. Sit and write all the souls of mankind, however many of them are born, and the places prepared for them to eternity; for all souls are prepared to eternity, before the formation of the world.

³And all double thirty days and thirty nights, and I wrote out all things exactly, and wrote three hundred and sixty-six books.

Chapter 24

[1]And the Lord summoned me, and said to me: Enoch, sit down on my left with Gabriel.

[2]And I bowed down to the Lord, and the Lord spoke to me: Enoch, beloved, all (that) you see, all things that are standing finished I tell to you even before the very beginning, all that I created from nonbeing, and visible (physical) things from invisible (spiritual).

[3]Hear, Enoch, and take in these my words, for not to My angels have I told my secret, and I have not told them their rise, nor my endless realm, nor have they understood my creating, which I tell you today.

[4]For before all things were visible (physical), I alone used to go about in the invisible (spiritual) things, like the sun from east to west, and from west to east.

[5]But even the sun has peace in itself, while I found no peace, because I was creating all things, and I conceived the thought of placing foundations, and of creating visible (physical) creation.

Chapter 25

[1]I commanded in the very lowest (parts), that visible (physical) things should come down from invisible (spiritual), and Adoil came down very great, and I beheld him, and lo! He had a belly of great light.

[2]And I said to him: Become undone, Adoil, and let the visible (physical) (come) out of you.

[3]And he came undone, and a great light came out. And I (was) in the midst of the great light, and as there is born light from light, there came forth a great age, and showed all creation, which I had thought to create.

[4]And I saw that (it was) good.

[5]And I placed for myself a throne, and took my seat on it, and said to the light: Go thence up higher and fix yourself high above the throne, and be A foundation to the highest things.

[6]And above the light there is nothing else, and then I bent up and looked up from my throne.

Chapter 26

[1]And I summoned the very lowest a second time, and said: Let Archas come forth hard, and he came forth hard from the invisible (spiritual).

[2]And Archas came forth, hard, heavy, and very red.

[3]And I said: Be opened, Archas, and let there be born from you, and he came undone, an age came forth, very great and very dark, bearing the creation of all lower things, and I saw that (it was) good and said to him:

[4]Go thence down below, and make yourself firm, and be a foundation for the lower things, and it happened and he went down and fixed himself, and became the foundation for the lower things, and below the darkness there is nothing else.

Chapter 27

[1]And I commanded that there should be taken from light and darkness, and I said: Be thick, and it became thus, and I spread it out with the light, and it became water, and I spread it out over the darkness, below the light, and then I made firm the waters, that is to say the bottomless, and I made foundation of light around the water, and created seven circles from inside, and imaged (the water) like crystal wet and dry, that is to say like glass, (and) the circumcision of the waters and the other elements, and I showed each one of them its road, and the seven stars each one of them in its heaven, that they go thus, and I saw that it was good.

[2]And I separated between light and between darkness, that is to say in the midst of the water hither and thither, and I said to the light, that it should be the day, and to the darkness, that it should be the night, and there was evening and there was morning the first day.

Chapter 28

[1]And then I made firm the heavenly circle, and (made) that the lower water which is under heaven collect itself together, into one whole, and that the chaos become dry, and it became so.

[2]Out of the waves I created rock hard and big, and from the rock I piled up the dry, and the dry I called earth, and the midst of the earth I called abyss, that is to say the bottomless, I collected the sea in one place and bound it together with a yoke.

[3]And I said to the sea: Behold I give you (your) eternal limits, and you shalt not break loose from your component parts.

[4]Thus I made fast the firmament. This day I called me the first-created [Sunday].

Chapter 29

[1]And for all the heavenly troops I imaged the image and essence of fire, and my eye looked at the very hard, firm rock, and from the gleam of my eye the lightning received its wonderful nature, (which) is both fire in water and water in fire, and one does not put out the other, nor does the one dry up the other, therefore the lightning is brighter than the sun, softer than water and firmer than hard rock.

[2]And from the rock I cut off a great fire, and from the fire I created the orders of the incorporeal ten troops of angels, and their weapons are fiery and their raiment a burning flame, and I commanded that each one should stand in his order.

[3]And one from out the order of angels, having turned away with the order that was under him, conceived an impossible thought, to place his throne higher than the clouds above the earth, that he might become equal in rank to my power.

[4]And I threw him out from the height with his angels, and he was flying in the air continuously above the bottomless.

Chapter 30

[1]On the third day I commanded the earth to make grow great and fruitful trees, and hills, and seed to sow, and I planted Paradise, and enclosed it, and placed as armed (guardians) flaming angels, and thus I created renewal.

[2]Then came evening, and came morning the fourth day.

[3][Wednesday]. On the fourth day I commanded that there should be great lights on the heavenly circles.

⁴On the first uppermost circle I placed the stars, Kruno, and on the second Aphrodit, on the third Aris, on the fifth Zoues, on the sixth Ermis, on the seventh lesser the moon, and adorned it with the lesser stars.

⁵And on the lower I placed the sun for the illumination of day, and the moon and stars for the illumination of night.

⁶The sun that it should go according to each constellation, twelve, and I appointed the succession of the months and their names and lives, their thunderings, and their hour-markings, how they should succeed.

⁷Then evening came and morning came the fifth day.

⁸[Thursday]. On the fifth day I commanded the sea, that it should bring forth fishes, and feathered birds of many varieties, and all animals creeping over the earth, going forth over the earth on four legs, and soaring in the air, male sex and female, and every soul breathing the spirit of life.

⁹And there came evening, and there came morning the sixth day.

¹⁰[Friday]. On the sixth day I commanded my wisdom to create man from seven consistencies: one, his flesh from the earth; two, his blood from the dew; three, his eyes from the sun; four, his bones from stone; five, his intelligence from the swiftness of the angels and from cloud; six, his veins and his hair from the grass of the earth; seven, his soul from my breath and from the wind.

¹¹And I gave him seven natures: to the flesh hearing, the eyes for sight, to the soul smell, the veins for touch, the blood for taste, the bones for endurance, to the intelligence sweetness [enjoyment].

¹²I conceived a cunning saying to say, I created man from invisible (spiritual) and from visible (physical) nature, of both are his death and life and image, he knows speech like some created thing, small in greatness and again great in smallness, and I placed him on earth, a second angel, honorable, great and glorious, and I appointed him as ruler to rule on earth and to have my wisdom, and there was none like him of earth of all my existing creatures.

¹³And I appointed him a name, from the four component parts, from east, from west, from south, from north, and I appointed for him four special stars, and I called his name Adam, and showed him the two ways, the light and the darkness, and I told him:

¹⁴This is good, and that bad, that I should learn whether he has love towards me, or hatred, that it be clear which in his race love me.

¹⁵For I have seen his nature, but he has not seen his own nature, therefore (through) not seeing he will sin worse, and I said After sin (what is there) but death?

[16]And I put sleep into him and he fell asleep. And I took from him A rib, and created him a wife, that death should come to him by his wife, and I took his last word and called her name mother, that is to say, Eva (Eve).

Chapter 31

[1]Adam has life on earth, and I created a garden in Eden in the east, that he should observe the testament and keep the command.

[2]I made the heavens open to him, that he should see the angels singing the song of victory, and the gloomless light.

[3]And he was continuously in paradise, and the devil understood that I wanted to create another world, because Adam was lord on earth, to rule and control it.

[4]The devil is the evil spirit of the lower places, as a fugitive he made Sotona from the heavens as his name was Satanail (Satan), thus he became different from the angels, (but his nature) did not change (his) intelligence as far as (his) understanding of righteous and sinful (things).

[5]And he understood his condemnation and the sin which he had sinned before, therefore he conceived thought against Adam, in such form he entered and seduced Eva (Eve), but did not touch Adam.

[6]But I cursed ignorance, but what I had blessed previously, those I did not curse, I cursed not man, nor the earth, nor other creatures, but man's evil fruit, and his works.

Chapter 32

[1]I said to him: Earth you are, and into the earth whence I took you you shalt go, and I will not ruin you, but send you whence I took you.

[2]Then I can again receive you at My second presence.

[3]And I blessed all my creatures visible (physical) and invisible (spiritual). And Adam was five and half hours in paradise.

[4]And I blessed the seventh day, which is the Sabbath, on which he rested from all his works.

Chapter 33

[1]And I appointed the eighth day also, that the eighth day should be the first-created after my work, and that (the first seven) revolve in the form of the seventh thousand, and that at the beginning of the eighth thousand there should be a time of not-counting, endless, with neither years nor months nor weeks nor days nor hours.

[2]And now, Enoch, all that I have told you, all that you have understood, all that you have seen of heavenly things, all that you have seen on earth, and all that I have written in books by my great wisdom, all these things I have devised and created from the uppermost foundation to the lower and to the end, and there is no counselor nor inheritor to my creations.

[3]I am self-eternal, not made with hands, and without change.

[4]My thought is my counselor, my wisdom and my word are made, and my eyes observe all things how they stand here and tremble with terror.

[5]If I turn away my face, then all things will be destroyed.

[6]And apply your mind, Enoch, and know him who is speaking to you, and take thence the books which you yourself have written.

[7]And I give you Samuil and Raguil, who led you up, and the books, and go down to earth, and tell your sons all that I have told you, and all that you have seen, from the lower heaven up to my throne, and all the troops.

[8]For I created all forces, and there is none that resists me or that does not subject himself to me. For all subject themselves to my monarchy, and labor for my sole rule.

[9]Give them the books of the handwriting, and they will read (them) and will know me for the creator of all things, and will understand how there is no other God but me.

[10]And let them distribute the books of your handwriting–children to children, generation to generation, nations to nations.

[11]And I will give you, Enoch, my intercessor, the archistratege Michael, for the handwritings of your fathers Adam, Seth, Enos, Cainan, Mahaleleel, and Jared your father.

Chapter 34

[1]They have rejected my commandments and my yoke, worthless seed has come up, not fearing God, and they would not bow down to me, but have begun to bow down to vain gods, and denied my unity, and have laden the whole earth with untruths, offences, abominable lecheries, namely one with another, and all manner of other unclean wickedness, which are disgusting to relate.

[2]And therefore I will bring down a deluge upon the earth and will destroy all men, and the whole earth will crumble together into great darkness.

Chapter 35

[1]Behold from their seed shall arise another generation, much afterwards, but of them many will be very insatiate.

[2]He who raises that generation, (shall) reveal to them the books of your handwriting, of your fathers, (to them) to whom he must point out the guardianship of the world, to the faithful men and workers of my pleasure, who do not acknowledge my name in vain.

[3]And they shall tell another generation, and those (others) having read shall be glorified thereafter, more than the first.

Chapter 36

[1]Now, Enoch, I give you the term of thirty days to spend in your house, and tell your sons and all your household, that all may hear from my face what is told them by you, that they may read and understand, how there is no other God but me.

[2]And that they may always keep my commandments, and begin to read and take in the books of your handwriting.

[3]And after thirty days I shall send my angel for you, and he will take you from earth and from your sons to me.

Chapter 37

[1]And the Lord called upon one of the older angels, terrible and menacing, and placed him by me, in appearance white as snow, and his hands like ice, having the appearance of great frost, and he froze my face, because I could not endure the terror of the Lord, just as it is not possible to endure A stove's fire and the sun's heat, and the frost of the air.

[2]And the Lord said to me: Enoch, if your face be not frozen here, no man will be able to behold your face.

Chapter 38

[1]And the Lord said to those men who first led me up: Let Enoch go down on to earth with you, and await him till the determined day.

[2]And they placed me by night on my bed.

[3]And Mathusal (Methuselah) expecting my coming, keeping watch by day and by night at my bed, was filled with awe when he heard my coming, and I told him, Let all my household come together, that I tell them everything.

Chapter 39

[1]Oh my children, my beloved ones, hear the admonition of your father, as much as is according to the Lord's will.

[2]I have been let come to you today, and announce to you, not from my lips, but from the Lord's lips, all that is and was and all that is now, and all that will be till judgment-day.

[3]For the Lord has let me come to you, you hear therefore the words of my lips, of a man made big for you, but I am one who has seen the Lord's face, like iron made to glow from fire it sends forth sparks and burns.

[4]You look now upon my eyes, (the eyes) of a man big with meaning for you, but I have seen the Lord's eyes, shining like the sun's rays and filling the eyes of man with awe.

⁵You see now, my children, the right hand of a man that helps you, but I have seen the Lord's right hand filling heaven as he helped me.

⁶You see the compass of my work like your own, but I have seen the Lord's limitless and perfect compass, which has no end.

⁷You hear the words of my lips, as I heard the words of the Lord, like great thunder incessantly with hurling of clouds.

⁸And now, my children, hear the discourses of the father of the earth, how fearful and awful it is to come before the face of the ruler of the earth, how much more terrible and awful it is to come before the face of the ruler of heaven, the controller (judge) of quick and dead, and of the heavenly troops. Who can endure that endless pain?

Chapter 40

¹And now, my children, I know all things, for this (is) from the Lord's lips, and this my eyes have seen, from beginning to end.

²I know all things, and have written all things into books, the heavens and their end, and their plenitude, and all the armies and their marchings.

³I have measured and described the stars, the great countless multitude (of them).

⁴What man has seen their revolutions, and their entrances? For not even the angels see their number, while I have written all their names.

⁵And I measured the sun's circle, and measured its rays, counted the hours, I wrote down too all things that go over the earth, I have written the things that are nourished, and all seed sown and unsown, which the earth produces and all plants, and every grass and every flower, and their sweet smells, and their names, and the dwelling-places of the clouds, and their composition, and their wings, and how they bear rain and raindrops.

⁶And I investigated all things, and wrote the road of the thunder and of the lightning, and they showed me the keys and their guardians, their rise, the way they go; it is let out (gently) in measure by a chain, lest by A heavy chain and violence it hurl down the angry clouds and destroy all things on earth.

⁷I wrote the treasure-houses of the snow, and the storehouses of the cold and the frosty airs, and I observed their season's key-holder, he fills the clouds with them, and does not exhaust the treasure-houses.

[8]And I wrote the resting-places of the winds and observed and saw how their key-holders bear weighing-scales and measures; first, they put them in (one) weighing-scale, then in the other the weights and let them out according to measure cunningly over the whole earth, lest by heavy breathing they make the earth to rock.

[9]And I measured out the whole earth, its mountains, and all hills, fields, trees, stones, rivers, all existing things I wrote down, the height from earth to the seventh heaven, and downwards to the very lowest hell, and the judgment-place, and the very great, open and weeping hell.

[10]And I saw how the prisoners are in pain, expecting the limitless judgment.

[11]And I wrote down all those being judged by the judge, and all their judgment (and sentences) and all their works.

Chapter 41

[1]And I saw all forefathers from (all) time with Adam and Eva (Eve), and I sighed and broke into tears and said of the ruin of their dishonor:

[2]Woe is me for my infirmity and (for that) of my forefathers, and thought in my heart and said:

[3]Blessed (is) the man who has not been born or who has been born and shall not sin before the Lord's face, that he come not into this place, nor bring the yoke of this place.

Chapter 42

[1]I saw the key-holders and guards of the gates of hell standing, like great serpents, and their faces like extinguishing lamps, and their eyes of fire, their sharp teeth, and I saw all the Lord's works, how they are right, while the works of man are some (good), and others bad, and in their works are known those who lie evilly.

Chapter 43

¹I, my children, measured and wrote out every work and every measure and every righteous judgment.

²As (one) year is more honorable than another, so is (one) man more honorable than another, some for great possessions, some for wisdom of heart, some for particular intellect, some for cunning, one for silence of lip, another for cleanliness, one for strength, another for comeliness, one for youth, another for sharp wit, one for shape of body, another for sensibility, let it be heard everywhere, but there is none better than he who fears God, he shall be more glorious in time to come.

Chapter 44

¹The Lord with his hands having created man, in the likeness of his own face, the Lord made him small and great.

²Whoever reviles the ruler's face, and abhors the Lord's face, has despised the Lord's face, and he who vents anger on any man without injury, the Lord's great anger will cut him down, he who spits on the face of man reproachfully, will be cut down at the Lord's great judgment.

³Blessed is the man who does not direct his heart with malice against any man, and helps the injured and condemned, and raises the broken down, and shall do charity to the needy, because on the day of the great judgment every weight, every measure and every makeweight (will be) as in the market, that is to say (they are) hung on scales and stand in the market, (and every one) shall learn his own measure, and according to his measure shall take his reward.

Chapter 45

¹Whoever hastens to make offerings before the Lord's face, the Lord for his part will hasten that offering by granting of his work.

²But whoever increases his lamp before the Lord's face and make not true judgment, the Lord will (not) increase his treasure in the realm of the highest.

[3]When the Lord demands bread, or candles, or (the)flesh (of beasts), or any other sacrifice, then that is nothing; but God demands pure hearts, and with all that (only) tests the heart of man.

Chapter 46

[1]Hear, my people, and take in the words of my lips.

[2]If any one bring any gifts to an earthly ruler, and have disloyal thoughts in his heart, and the ruler know this, will he not be angry with him, and not refuse his gifts, and not give him over to judgment?

[3]Or (if) one man make himself appear good to another by deceit of tongue, but (have) evil in his heart, then will not (the other) understand the treachery of his heart, and himself be condemned, since his untruth was plain to all?

[4]And when the Lord shall send a great light, then there will be judgment for the just and the unjust, and there no one shall escape notice.

Chapter 47

[1]And now, my children, lay thought on your hearts, mark well the words of your father, which are all (come) to you from the Lord's lips.

[2]Take these books of your father's handwriting and read them.

[3]For the books are many, and in them you will learn all the Lord's works, all that has been from the beginning of creation, and will be till the end of time.

[4]And if you will observe my handwriting, you will not sin against the Lord; because there is no other except the Lord, neither in heaven, nor in earth, nor in the very lowest (places), nor in the (one) foundation.

[5]The Lord has placed the foundations in the unknown, and has spread forth heavens visible (physical) and invisible (spiritual); he fixed the earth on the waters, and created countless creatures, and who has counted the water and the foundation of the unfixed, or the dust of the earth, or the sand of the sea, or the drops of the rain, or the morning dew, or the wind's breathings? Who has filled earth and sea, and the indissoluble winter?

[6]I cut the stars out of fire, and decorated heaven, and put it in their midst.

Chapter 48

[1]That the sun go along the seven heavenly circles, which are the appointment of one hundred and eighty-two thrones, that it go down on a short day, and again one hundred and eighty-two, that it go down on a big day, and he has two thrones on which he rests, revolving hither and thither above the thrones of the months, from the seventeenth day of the month Tsivan it goes down to the month Thevan, from the seventeenth of Thevan it goes up.

[2]And thus it goes close to the earth, then the earth is glad and makes grow its fruits, and when it goes away, then the earth is sad, and trees and all fruits have no florescence.

[3]All this he measured, with good measurement of hours, and fixed A measure by his wisdom, of the visible (physical) and the invisible (spiritual).

[4]From the invisible (spiritual) he made all things visible (physical), himself being invisible (spiritual).

[5]Thus I make known to you, my children, and distribute the books to your children, into all your generations, and amongst the nations who shall have the sense to fear God, let them receive them, and may they come to love them more than any food or earthly sweets, and read them and apply themselves to them.

[6]And those who understand not the Lord, who fear not God, who accept not, but reject, who do not receive the (books), a terrible judgment awaits these.

[7]Blessed is the man who shall bear their yoke and shall drag them along, for he shall be released on the day of the great judgment.

Chapter 49

[1]I swear to you, my children, but I swear not by any oath, neither by heaven nor by earth, nor by any other creature which God created.

[2]The Lord said: There is no oath in me, nor injustice, but truth.

[3]If there is no truth in men, let them swear by the words, Yea, yea, or else, Nay, nay.

[4]And I swear to you, yea, yea, that there has been no man in his mother's womb, (but that) already before, even to each one there is a place prepared for the repose of that soul, and a measure fixed how much it is intended that a man be tried in this world.

[5]Yea, children, deceive not yourselves, for there has been previously prepared a place for every soul of man.

Chapter 50

[1]I have put every man's work in writing and none born on earth can remain hidden nor his works remain concealed.

[2]I see all things.

[3]Now therefore, my children, in patience and meekness spend the number of your days, that you inherit endless life.

[4]Endure for the sake of the Lord every wound, every injury, every evil word and attack.

[5]If ill-requitals befall you, return (them) not either to neighbor or enemy, because the Lord will return (them) for you and be your avenger on the day of great judgment, that there be no avenging here among men.

[6]Whoever of you spends gold or silver for his brother's sake, he will receive ample treasure in the world to come.

[7]Injure not widows nor orphans nor strangers, lest God's wrath come upon you.

Chapter 51

[1]Stretch out your hands to the poor according to your strength.

[2]Hide not your silver in the earth.

[3]Help the faithful man in affliction, and affliction will not find you in the time of your trouble.

[4]And every grievous and cruel yoke that come upon you bear all for the sake of the Lord, and thus you will find your reward in the day of judgment.

[5]It is good to go morning, midday, and evening into the Lord's dwelling, for the glory of your creator.

[6]Because every breathing (thing) glorifies him, and every creature visible (physical) and invisible (spiritual) returns him praise.

Chapter 52

[1]Blessed is the man who opens his lips in praise of God of Sabaoth and praises the Lord with his heart.

[2]Cursed every man who opens his lips for the bringing into contempt and calumny of his neighbor, because he brings God into contempt.

[3]Blessed is he who opens his lips blessing and praising God.

[4]Cursed is he before the Lord all the days of his life, who opens his lips to curse and abuse.

[5]Blessed is he who blesses all the Lord's works.

[6]Cursed is he who brings the Lord's creation into contempt.

[7]Blessed is he who looks down and raises the fallen.

[8]Cursed is he who looks to and is eager for the destruction of what is not his.

[9]Blessed is he who keeps the foundations of his fathers made firm from the beginning.

[10]Cursed is he who perverts the decrees of his forefathers.

[11]Blessed is he who imparts peace and love.

[12]Cursed is he who disturbs those that love their neighbors.

[13]Blessed is he who speaks with humble tongue and heart to all.

[14]Cursed is he who speaks peace with his tongue, while in his heart there is no peace but a sword.

[15]For all these things will be laid bare in the weighing-scales and in the books, on the day of the great judgment.

Chapter 53

[1]And now, my children, do not say: Our father is standing before God, and is praying for our sins, for there is there no helper of any man who has sinned.

[2]You see how I wrote all works of every man, before his creation, (all) that is done amongst all men for all time, and none can tell or relate my handwriting, because the Lord see all imaginings of man, how they are vain, where they lie in the treasure-houses of the heart.

[3]And now, my children, mark well all the words of your father, that I tell you, lest you regret, saying: Why did our father not tell us?

Chapter 54

[1]At that time, not understanding this let these books which I have given you be for an inheritance of your peace.

[2]Hand them to all who want them, and instruct them, that they may see the Lord's very great and marvelous works.

Chapter 55

[1]My children, behold, the day of my term and time have approached.

[2]For the angels who shall go with me are standing before me and urge me to my departure from you; they are standing here on earth, awaiting what has been told them.

[3]For tomorrow I shall go up on to heaven, to the uppermost Jerusalem to my eternal inheritance.

[4]Therefore I bid you do before the Lord's face all (his) good pleasure.

Chapter 56

[1]Mathosalam having answered his father Enoch, said: What is agreeable to your eyes, father, that I may make before your face, that you may bless our dwellings, and your sons, and that your people may be made glorious through you, and then (that) you may depart thus, as the Lord said?

[2]Enoch answered to his son Mathosalam (and) said: Hear, child, from the time when the Lord anointed me with the ointment of his glory, (there has been no) food in me, and my soul remembers not earthly enjoyment, neither do I want anything earthly.

Chapter 57

[1]My child Methosalam, summon all your brethren and all your household and the elders of the people, that I may talk to them and depart, as is planned for me.

[2]And Methosalam made haste, and summoned his brethren, Regim, Riman, Uchan, Chermion, Gaidad, and all the elders of the people before the face of his father Enoch; and he blessed them, (and) said to them:

Chapter 58

[1]Listen to me, my children, today.

[2]In those days when the Lord came down on to earth for Adam's sake, and visited all his creatures, which he created himself, after all these he created Adam, and the Lord called all the beasts of the earth, all the reptiles, and all the birds that soar in the air, and brought them all before the face of our father Adam.

[3]And Adam gave the names to all things living on earth.

[4]And the Lord appointed him ruler over all, and subjected to him all things under his hands, and made them dumb and made them dull that they be commanded of man, and be in subjection and obedience to him.

[5]Thus also the Lord created every man lord over all his possessions.

[6]The Lord will not judge a single soul of beast for man's sake, but adjudges the souls of men to their beasts in this world; for men have a special place.

[7]And as every soul of man is according to number, similarly beasts will not perish, nor all souls of beasts which the Lord created, till the great judgment, and they will accuse man, if he feed them ill.

Chapter 59

[1]Whoever defiles the soul of beasts, defiles his own soul.

[2]For man brings clean animals to make sacrifice for sin, that he may have cure of his soul.

[3]And if they bring for sacrifice clean animals, and birds, man has cure, he cures his soul.

[4]All is given you for food, bind it by the four feet, that is to make good the cure, he cures his soul.

[5]But whoever kills beast without wounds, kills his own souls and defiles his own flesh.

[6]And he who does any beast any injury whatsoever, in secret, it is evil practice, and he defiles his own soul.

Chapter 60

[1]He who works the killing of a man's soul, kills his own soul, and kills his own body, and there is no cure for him for all time.

[2]He who puts a man in any snare, shall stick in it himself, and there is no cure for him for all time.

[3]He who puts a man in any vessel, his retribution will not be wanting at the great judgment for all time.

[4]He who works crookedly or speaks evil against any soul, will not make justice for himself for all time.

Chapter 61

[1]And now, my children, keep your hearts from every injustice, which the Lord hates. Just as a man asks something for his own soul from God, so let him do to every living soul, because I know all things, how in the great time to come there is much inheritance prepared for men, good for the good, and bad for the bad, without number many.

[2]Blessed are those who enter the good houses, for in the bad houses there is no peace nor return from them.

[3]Hear, my children, small and great! When man puts a good thought in his heart, brings gifts from his labors before the Lord's face and his hands made them not, then the Lord will turn away his face from the labor of his hand, and (that) man cannot find the labor of his hands.

[4]And if his hands made it, but his heart murmur, and his heart cease not making murmur incessantly, he has not any advantage.

Chapter 62

[1]Blessed is the man who in his patience brings his gifts with faith before the Lord's face, because he will find forgiveness of sins.

[2]But if he take back his words before the time, there is no repentance for him; and if the time pass and he do not of his own will what is promised, there is no repentance after death.

[3]Because every work which man does before the time, is all deceit before men, and sin before God.

Chapter 63

[1]When man clothes the naked and fills the hungry, he will find reward from God.

[2]But if his heart murmur, he commits a double evil; ruin of himself and of that which he gives; and for him there will be no finding of reward on account of that.

[3]And if his own heart is filled with his food and his own flesh, clothed with his own clothing, he commits contempt, and will forfeit all his endurance of poverty, and will not find reward of his good deeds.

[4]Every proud and magniloquent man is hateful to the Lord, and every false speech, clothed in untruth; it will be cut with the blade of the sword of death, and thrown into the fire, and shall burn for all time.

Chapter 64

[1]When Enoch had spoken these words to his sons, all people far and near heard how the Lord was calling Enoch. They took counsel together:

[2]Let us go and kiss Enoch, and two thousand men came together and came to the place Achuzan where Enoch was, and his sons.

[3]And the elders of the people, the whole assembly, came and bowed down and began to kiss Enoch and said to him:

[4]Our father Enoch, (may) you (be) blessed of the Lord, the eternal ruler, and now bless your sons and all the people, that we may be glorified today before your face.

[5]For you shalt be glorified before the Lord's face for all time, since the Lord chose you, rather than all men on earth, and designated you writer of all his creation, visible (physical) and invisible (spiritual), and redeemed of the sins of man, and helper of your household.

Chapter 65

[1]And Enoch answered all his people saying: Hear, my children, before that all creatures were created, the Lord created the visible (physical) and invisible (spiritual) things.

[2]And as much time as there was and went past, understand that after all that he created man in the likeness of his own form, and put into him eyes to see, and ears to hear, and heart to reflect, and intellect wherewith to deliberate.

[3]And the Lord saw all man's works, and created all his creatures, and divided time, from time he fixed the years, and from the years he appointed the months, and from the months he appointed the days, and of days he appointed seven.

[4]And in those he appointed the hours, measured them out exactly, that man might reflect on time and count years, months, and hours, (their) alternation, beginning, and end, and that he might count his own life, from the beginning until death, and reflect on his sin and write his work bad and good; because no work is hidden before the Lord, that every man might know his works and never transgress all his commandments, and keep my handwriting from generation to generation.

[5]When all creation visible (physical) and invisible (spiritual), as the Lord created it, shall end, then every man goes to the great judgment, and then all time shall perish, and the years, and thenceforward there will be neither months nor days nor hours, they will be adhered together and will not be counted.

[6]There will be one eon, and all the righteous who shall escape the Lord's great judgment, shall be collected in the great eon, for the righteous the great eon will begin, and they will live eternally, and then too there will be amongst them neither labor, nor sickness, nor humiliation, nor anxiety, nor need, nor brutality, nor night, nor darkness, but great light.

[7]And they shall have a great indestructible wall, and a paradise bright and incorruptible (eternal), for all corruptible (mortal) things shall pass away, and there will be eternal life.

Chapter 66

[1]And now, my children, keep your souls from all injustice, such as the Lord hates.

[2]Walk before his face with terror and trembling and serve him alone.

[3]Bow down to the true God, not to dumb idols, but bow down to his similitude, and bring all just offerings before the Lord's face. The Lord hates what is unjust.

[4]For the Lord sees all things; when man takes thought in his heart, then he counsels the intellects, and every thought is always before the Lord, who made firm the earth and put all creatures on it.

[5]If you look to heaven, the Lord is there; if you take thought of the sea's deep and all the under-earth, the Lord is there.

[6]For the Lord created all things. Bow not down to things made by man, leaving the Lord of all creation, because no work can remain hidden before the Lord's face.

[7]Walk, my children, in longsuffering, in meekness, honesty, in provocation, in grief, in faith and in truth, in (reliance on) promises, in illness, in abuse, in wounds, in temptation, in nakedness, in privation, loving one another, till you go out from this age of ills, that you become inheritors of endless time.

[8]Blessed are the just who shall escape the great judgment, for they shall shine forth more than the sun sevenfold, for in this world the seventh part is taken off from all, light, darkness, food, enjoyment, sorrow, paradise, torture, fire, frost, and other things; he put all down in writing, that you might read and understand.

Chapter 67

[1]When Enoch had talked to the people, the Lord sent out darkness on to the earth, and there was darkness, and it covered those men standing with Enoch, and they took Enoch up on to the highest heaven, where the Lord (is); and he received him and placed him before his face, and the darkness went off from the earth, and light came again.

[2]And the people saw and understood not how Enoch had been taken, and glorified God, and found a roll in which was traced The Invisible (spiritual) God; and all went to their dwelling places.

Chapter 68

¹Enoch was born on the sixth day of the month Tsivan, and lived three hundred and sixty-five years.

²He was taken up to heaven on the first day of the month Tsivan and remained in heaven sixty days.

³He wrote all these signs of all creation, which the Lord created, and wrote three hundred and sixty-six books, and handed them over to his sons and remained on earth thirty days, and was again taken up to heaven on the sixth day of the month Tsivan, on the very day and hour when he was born.

⁴As every man's nature in this life is dark, so are also his conception, birth, and departure from this life.

⁵At what hour he was conceived, at that hour he was born, and at that hour too he died.

⁶Methosalam and his brethren, all the sons of Enoch, made haste, and erected an altar at that place called Achuzan, whence and where Enoch had been taken up to heaven.

⁷And they took sacrificial oxen and summoned all people and sacrificed the sacrifice before the Lord's face.

⁸All people, the elders of the people and the whole assembly came to the feast and brought gifts to the sons of Enoch.

⁹And they made a great feast, rejoicing and making merry three days, praising God, who had given them such a sign through Enoch, who had found favor with him, and that they should hand it on to their sons from generation to generation, from age to age.

¹⁰Amen.

Hebrew Book of Enoch

by

R. ISHMAEL BEN ELISHA
THE HIGH PRIEST

CHAPTER 1

INTRODUCTION: R. Ishmael ascends heaven to behold the vision of the Merkaba and is given in charge to Metatron

AND ENOCH WALKED WITH GOD: AND HE WAS NOT FOR; GOD TOOK HIM

(Gen. 5:24)

Rabbi Ishmael said:

(1)When I ascended on high to behold the vision of the *Merkaba* and had entered the six Halls, one within the other: (2)as soon as I reached the door of the seventh Hall I stood still in prayer before the Holy One, blessed be He, and, lifting up my eyes on high (i.e. towards the Divine Majesty), I said: (3)"Lord of the Universe, I pray thee, that the merit of Aaron, the son of Amram, the lover of peace and pursuer of peace, who received the crown of priesthood from Thy Glory on the mount of Sinai, be valid for me in this hour, so that *Qafsiel*, the prince, and the angels with him may not get power over me nor throw me down from the heavens".

(4)Forthwith the Holy One, blessed be He, sent to me Metatron, his Servant (*'Ebed*) the angel, the Prince of the Presence, and he, spreading his wings, with great joy came to meet me so as to save me from their hand.

(5)And he took me by his hand in their sight, saying to me: "Enter in peace before the high and exalted King and behold the picture of the *Merkaba*".

(6)Then I entered the seventh Hall, and he led me to the camp(s) of *Shekina* and placed me before the Holy One, blessed be He, to behold the *Merkaba*.

(7)As soon as the princes of the *Merkaba* and the flaming *Seraphim* perceived me, they fixed their eyes upon me. Instantly trembling and shuddering seized me and I fell down and was benumbed by the radiant image of their eyes and the splendid appearance of their faces; until the Holy One, blessed be He, rebuked them, saying:

(8)"My servants, my *Seraphim*, my *Kerubim* and my *'Ophannim*! Cover ye your eyes before Ishmael, my son, my friend, my beloved one and my glory, that he tremble not nor shudder!" (9)Forthwith Metatron the Prince of the Presence, came and restored my spirit and put me upon my feet. (10)After that (moment) there was not in me strength enough to say a song before the Throne of Glory of the glorious King, the mightiest of all kings, the most excellent of all princes, until after the hour had passed.

(11)After one hour (had passed) the Holy One, blessed be He, opened to me the gates of *Shekina*, the gates of Peace, the gates of Wisdom, the gates of Strength, the gates of Power, the gates of Speech (*Dibbur*), the gates of Song, the gates of *Qedushsha*, the gates of Chant.

(12)And he enlightened my eyes and my heart by words of psalm, song, praise, exaltation, thanksgiving, extolment, glorification, hymn and eulogy. And as I opened my mouth, uttering a song before the Holy One, blessed be He, the Holy *Chayyoth* beneath and above the Throne of Glory answered and said: "HOLY" and "BLESSED BE THE GLORY OF YHWH FROM HIS PLACE!" (i.e. chanted the *Qedushsha*).

CHAPTER 2

The highest classes of angels make inquiries about R. Ishmael,
which are answered by Metatron

R. Ishmael said:

(1)In that hour the eagles of the *Merkaba*, the flaming 'Ophannim and the *Seraphim* of consuming fire asked Metatron, saying to him:

(2)"Youth! Why sufferest thou one born of woman to enter and behold the *Merkaba*? From which nation, from which tribe is this one? What is his character?"

(3)Metatron answered and said to them:

"From the nation of Israel whom the Holy One, blessed be He, chose for his people from among seventy tongues (nations), from the tribe of Levi, whom he set aside as a contribution to his name and from the seed of Aaron whom the Holy One, blessed be He, did choose for his servant and put upon him the crown of priesthood on Sinai".

(4)Forthwith they spake and said:

"Indeed, this one is worthy to behold the *Merkaba* ". And they said: "Happy is the people that is in such a case!" (Ps. 144:15).

CHAPTER 3

Metatron has 70 names, but God calls him 'Youth'

R. Ishmael said:

(1)In that hour I asked Metatron, the angel, the Prince of the Presence: "What is thy name?" (2)He answered me: "I have seventy names, corresponding to the seventy tongues of the world and all of them are based upon the name Metatron, angel of the Presence; but my King calls me 'Youth' (*Na'ar*)"

CHAPTER 4

Metatron is identical with Enoch who was translated to heaven at the time of the Deluge

R. Ishmael said:

(1)I asked Metatron and said to him: "Why art thou called by the name of thy Creator, by seventy names? Thou art greater than all the princes, higher than all the angels, beloved more than all the servants, honored above all the mighty ones in kingship, greatness and glory: why do they call thee 'Youth' in the high heavens?"

(2)He answered and said to me: "Because I am Enoch, the son of Jared. (3)For when the generation of the flood sinned and were confounded in their deeds, saying unto God: 'Depart from us, for we desire not the knowledge of thy ways (Job 21:14)', then the Holy One, blessed be He, removed me from their midst to be a witness against them in the high heavens to all the inhabitants of the world, that they may not say: 'The Merciful One is cruel'.

(4)*ADEL:*

BC:

What sinned all those multitudes, their wives, their sons and their daughters, their horses, their mules and their cattle and their property, and all the birds of the world, all of which the Holy One, blessed be He, destroyed from the world together with them in the waters of the flood?

What sins had they committed, all those multitudes? Or, let it be they sinned, what had their sons and their daughters, their mules and their cattle sinned? And likewise, all the animals, domestic and wild, and the birds in the

ADL:	E:	BC:
Nor may say: What though the generation of the flood did sin; the beasts and the birds, what had they sinned, that they should perish with them?'	what had they sinned that they should perish with them ?'	world that God did destroy from the world?'

(5)Hence the Holy One, blessed be He, lifted me up in their lifetime before their eyes to be a witness against them to the future world. And the Holy One, blessed be He, assigned me for a prince and a ruler among the ministering angels.

(6)In that hour three of the ministering angels, 'UZZA, 'AZZA and 'AZZAEL came forth and brought charges against me in the high heavens, saying before the Holy One, blessed be He: "Said not the Ancient Ones (First Ones) rightly before Thee: 'Do not create man!'" The Holy One, blessed be He, answered and said unto them: "I have made and I will bear, yea, I will carry and will deliver". (Is. 46:4.)

(7)As soon as they saw me, they said before Him: "Lord of the Universe! What is this one that he should ascend to the height of heights? Is not he one from among the sons of [the sons of] those who perished in the days of the Flood? "What doeth he in the *Raqia*?"

(8)Again, the Holy One, blessed be He, answered and said to them: "What are ye, that ye enter and speak in my presence? I delight in this one more than in all of you, and hence he shall be a prince and a ruler over you in the high heavens." (9)Forthwith all stood up and went out to meet me, prostrated themselves before me and said: "Happy art thou and happy is thy father for thy Creator doth favor thee".

(10)And because I am small and a youth among them in days, months and years, therefore they call me "Youth" (*Na'ar*).

CHAPTER 5

The idolatry of the generation of Enosh causes God to remove the Shekina from earth. The idolatry inspired by 'Azza, 'Uzza and 'Azziel

R. Ishmael said: Metatron, the Prince of the Presence, said to me:

(1)From the day when the Holy One, blessed be He, expelled the first Adam from the Garden of Eden (and onwards), *Shekina* was dwelling upon a *Kerub* under the Tree of Life.

(2)And the ministering angels were gathering together and going down from heaven in parties, from the *Raqia* in companies and from the heavens in camps to do His will in the whole world.

(3)And the first man and his generation were sitting outside the gate of the Garden to behold the radiant appearance of the *Shekina*.

(4)For the splendor of the *Shekina* traversed the world from one end to the other (with a splendor) 365,000 times (that) of the globe of the sun. And everyone who made use of the splendor of the *Shekina*, on him no flies and no gnats did rest, neither was he ill nor suffered he any pain. No demons got power over him, neither were they able to injure him.

(5)When the Holy One, blessed be He, went out and went in: from the Garden to Eden, from Eden to the Garden, from the Garden to *Raqia* and from *Raqia* to the Garden of Eden then all and everyone beheld the splendor of His *Shekina* and they were not injured; (6)until the time of the generation of Enosh who was the head of all idol worshippers of the world. (7)And what did the generation of Enosh do? They went from one end of the world to the other, and each one brought silver, gold, precious stones and pearls in heaps like unto mountains and hills making idols out of them throughout all the world. And they erected the idols in every quarter of the world: the size of each idol was 1000 parasangs. (8)And they brought down the sun, the moon, planets and constellations, and placed them before the idols on their right hand and on their left, to attend them even as they attend the Holy One, blessed be He, as it is written (1 Kings 22:19): "And all the host of heaven was standing by him on his right hand and on his left".

(9)What power was in them that they were able to bring them down? They would not have been able to bring them down but for 'UZZA, 'AZZA and 'AZZIEL who taught them "sorceries whereby they brought them down and made use of them.

(10)In that time the ministering angels brought charges (against them) before the Holy One, blessed be He, saying before him: "Master of the World! What hast thou to do with the children of men? As it is written (Ps. 8:4) 'What is man (Enosh) that thou art mindful of him?' 'Mah Adam' is not written here, but 'Mah Enosh', for he (Enosh) is the head of the idol worshippers, (11)Why hast thou left

ADE:	*B:*	*CL:*
the highest of the high	the *'Araboth Raqia* which	the highest of the high

heavens, the abode of thy glorious Name, and the high and exalted Throne in 'Araboth on high	are full of thy glory, mighty and high alike, and the high and exalted Throne in the 'Araboth Raqia in the highest	heavens which are filled with the majesty of thy glory and are high, up lifted and exalted, and the high and exalted Throne in the Raqia 'Araboth on high

and art gone and dwellest with the children of men who worship idols and equal thee to the idols. (12)Now thou art on earth and the idols likewise. What hast thou to do with the inhabitants of the earth who worship idols?" (13)Forthwith the Holy One, blessed be He, lifted up His *Shekina* from the earth, from their midst.

(14)In that moment came the ministering angels, the troops of hosts and the armies of 'Araboth in thousand camps and ten thousand hosts: they fetched trumpets and took the horns in their hands and surrounded the *Shekina* with all kinds of songs. And He ascended to the high heavens, as it is written (Ps. 47:5): "God is gone up with a shout, the Lord with the sound of a trumpet ".

CHAPTER 6

Enoch lifted up to heaven together with the Shekina. Angels'
protests answered by God

R. Ishmael said: Metatron, the Angel, the Prince of the Presence, said to me:

(1)When the Holy One, blessed be He, desired to lift me up on high, He first sent *Anaphiel* H (H = *Tetragrammaton*), the Prince, and he took me from their midst in their sight and carried me in great glory upon a fiery chariot with fiery horses, servants of glory. And he lifted me up to the high heavens together with the *Shekina*.

(2)As soon as I reached the high heavens, the Holy *Chayyoth*, the 'Ophannim, the *Seraphim*, the *Kerubim*, the Wheels of the *Merkaba* (the Galgallim), and the ministers of the consuming fire, perceiving my smell from a distance of 365,000 myriads of parasangs, said:

A:	B:	CDEL:
"What smell of one born of woman and what taste of a white drop (is this) that	"What is one born of woman between (among) us? The taste of a white	"What smell of a woman-born is this and what taste of a white drop that

ascends on high, and (lo, he is merely) a gnat among those who ' divide flames (of fire)'?" drop which ascends to the high heavens to minister among those who 'divide flames of fire'". ascends to the high heavens to minister among dividers of flames.

(3)The Holy One, blessed be He, answered and spake unto them: "My servants, my hosts, my *Kerubim*, my '*Ophannim*, my *Seraphim*! Be ye not displeased on account of this! Since all the children of men have denied me and my great Kingdom and are gone worshipping idols, I have removed my *Shekina* from among them and have lifted it up on high. But this one whom I have taken from among them is an ELECT ONE among (the inhabitants of) the world and he is equal to all of them in faith, righteousness and perfection of deed and I have taken him for (as) a tribute from my world under all the heavens".

CHAPTER 7

Enoch raised upon the wings of the Shekina to the place of the Throne, the Merkaba and the angelic hosts

R. Ishmael said: Metatron, the Angel, the Prince of the Presence, said to me:

When the Holy One, blessed be He, took me away from the generation of the Flood, he lifted me on the wings of the wind of *Shekina* to the highest heaven and brought me into the great palaces of the '*Araboth Raqia* on high, where are the glorious Throne of *Shekina*, the *Merkaba*, the troops of anger, the armies of vehemence, the fiery *Shin'anim*', the flaming *Kerubim*, and the burning '*Ophannim*, the flaming servants, the flashing *Chashmallim* and the lightening *Seraphim*. And he placed me (there) to attend the Throne of Glory day after day.

CHAPTER 8

The gates (of the treasuries of heaven) opened to Metatron

R. Ishmael said: Metatron, the Prince of the Presence, said to me:

(1)Before He appointed me to attend the Throne of Glory, the Holy One, blessed be He, opened to me

three hundred thousand gates of Understanding
three hundred thousand gates of Subtlety
three hundred thousand gates of Life
three hundred thousand gates of 'grace and loving-kindness'
three hundred thousand gates of love
three hundred thousand gates of Tora
three hundred thousand gates of meekness
three hundred thousand gates of maintenance
three hundred thousand gates of mercy
three hundred thousand gates of fear of heaven.

(2)In that hour the Holy One, blessed be He, added in me wisdom unto wisdom, understanding unto understanding, subtlety unto subtlety, knowledge unto knowledge, mercy unto mercy, instruction unto instruction, love unto love, loving-kindness unto loving-kindness, goodness unto goodness, meekness unto meekness, power unto power, strength unto strength, might unto might, brilliance unto brilliance, beauty unto beauty, splendor unto splendor, and I was honored and adorned with all these good and praiseworthy things more than all the children of heaven.

CHAPTER 9

Enoch receives blessings from the Most High and is adorned
with angelic attributes

R. Ishmael said: Metatron, the Prince of the Presence, said to me:

(1)After all these things the Holy One, blessed be He, put His hand upon me and blessed me with 5360 blessings. (2)And I was raised and enlarged to the size of the length and width of the world.

(3)And He caused 72 wings to grow on me, 36 on each side. And each wing was as the whole world. (4)And He fixed on me 365 eyes: each eye was as the great luminary. (5)And He left no kind of splendor, brilliance, radiance, beauty in (of) all the lights of the universe that He did not fix on me.

CHAPTER 10

God places Metatron on a throne at the door of the seventh Hall and announces through the Herald, that Metatron henceforth is God's representative and ruler over all the princes of kingdoms and all the children of heaven, save the eight high princes called YHWH by the name of their King

R. Ishmael said: Metatron, the Prince of the Presence, said to me:

(1)All these things the Holy One, blessed be He, made for me: He made me a Throne, similar to the Throne of Glory. And He spread over me a curtain of splendor and brilliant appearance, of beauty, grace and mercy, similar to the curtain of the Throne of Glory; and on it were fixed all kinds of lights in the universe.

(2)And He placed it at the door of the Seventh Hall and seated me on it.

(3)And the herald went forth into every heaven, saying: This is Metatron, my servant. I have made him into a prince and a ruler over all the princes of my kingdoms and over all the children of heaven, *except the eight great princes, the honored and revered ones who are called YHWH, by the name of their King.* (4)And every angel and every prince who has a word to speak in my presence (before me) shall go into his presence (before him) and shall speak to him (instead). (5)And every command that he utters to you in my name do ye observe and fulfill. For the Prince of Wisdom and the Prince of Understanding have I committed to him to instruct him in the wisdom of heavenly things and of earthly things, in the wisdom of this world and of the world to come. (6)Moreover, I have set him over all the treasuries of the palaces of *Araboth* and over all the stores of life that I have in the high heavens.

CHAPTER 11

God reveals all mysteries and secrets to Metatron

R. Ishmael said: Metatron, the angel, the Prince of the Presence, said to me:

(1)Henceforth the Holy One, blessed be He, revealed to me all the mysteries of Tora and all the secrets of wisdom and all the depths of the Perfect Law; and all living beings' thoughts of heart and all the secrets of the universe and all the secrets of Creation were revealed unto me even as they are revealed unto the Maker of Creation.

(2)And I watched intently to behold the secrets of the depth and the wonderful mystery.

ABL: *C:*

Before a man did think 8 in secret, I saw   Before a man did think, I knew what was
(it) and before a man made a thing I   in his thought. (3)And there was nothing
beheld it. (3)And there was nothing on   above on high nor below in the deep
high nor in the depth of the world hidden   hidden from me.
from me.

CHAPTER 12

*God clothes Metatron in a garment of glory, puts a royal
crown on his head and calls him "the Lesser YHWH"*

R. Ishmael said: Metatron, the Prince of the Presence, said to me:

(1)By reason of the love with which the Holy One, blessed be He, loved me more than all the children of heaven, He made me a garment of glory on which were fixed all kinds of lights, and He clad me in it. (2)And He made me a robe of honor on which were fixed all kinds of beauty, splendor, brilliance and majesty. (3)And he made me a royal crown in which were fixed forty-nine costly stones like unto the light of the globe of the sun. (4)For its splendor went forth in the four quarters of the 'Araboth Raqia, and in (through) the seven heavens, and in the four quarters of the world. And he put it on my head.

(5)And He called me THE LESSER YHWH in the presence of all His heavenly household; as it is written (Ex. 23:21): "For my name is in him".

CHAPTER 13

*God writes with a flaming style on Metatron's crown the
cosmic letters by which heaven and earth were created*

R. Ishmael said: Metatron, the angel, the Prince of the Presence, the Glory of all heavens, said to me:

(1)Because of the great love and mercy with which the Holy One, blessed be He, loved and cherished me more than all the children of heaven, He wrote with his ringer with a flaming style upon the crown on my head the letters by which were created heaven and earth, the seas and rivers, the mountains and hills, the planets and constellations, the lightnings, winds, earthquakes and voices (thunders), the snow and hail, the storm-wind and the tempest; the letters by which were created all the needs of the world and all the orders of Creation.

(2)And every single letter sent forth time after time as it were "lightnings, time after time as it were torches, time after time as it were flames of fire, time after time (rays) like [as] the rising of the sun and the moon and the planets.

CHAPTER 14

All the highest princes, the elementary angels and the
planetary and sideric angels fear and tremble at the sight of
Metatron crowned

R. Ishmael said: Metatron, the Angel, the Prince of the Presence, said to me:

(1)When the Holy One, blessed be He, put this crown on my head, (then) trembled before me all the Princes of Kingdoms who are in the height of 'Araboth Raqia and all the hosts of every heaven; and even the princes (of) the 'Elim, the princes (of) the 'Er'ellim and the princes (of) the *Tafsarim*, who are greater than all the ministering angels who minister before the Throne of Glory, shook, feared and trembled before me when they beheld me.

(2)Even Sammael, the Prince of the Accusers, who is greater than all the princes of kingdoms on high; feared and trembled before me.

(3)And even the angel of fire, and the angel of hail, and the angel of the wind, and the angel of the lightning, and the angel of anger, and the angel of the thunder, and the angel of the snow, and the angel of the rain; and the angel of the day, and the angel of the night, and the angel of the sun and the angel of the moon and the angel of the planets and the angel of the constellations who rule the world under their hands, feared and trembled and were affrighted before me, when they beheld me.

(4)These are the names of the rulers of the world: *Gabriel*, the angel of the fire, *Baradiel*, the angel of the hail, *Ruchiel* who is appointed over the wind, *Baraqiel* who is appointed over the lightnings, *Za'amiel* who is appointed over the vehemence, *Ziqiel* who is appointed over the sparks, *Zi'iel* who is appointed over the commotion, *Za'aphiel* who is appointed over the storm-wind, *Ra'amiel* who is appointed over the thunders, *Ra'ashiel* who is appointed over the earthquake, *Shalgiel* who is appointed over the snow, *Matariel* who is appointed over the rain, *Shimshiel* who is appointed over the day, *Lailiel* who is appointed over the night, *Galgalliel* who is appointed over the globe of the sun, *'Ophanniel* who is appointed over the globe of the moon, *Kokbiel* who is appointed over the planets, *Rahatiel* who is appointed over the constellations.

(5) And they all fell prostrate, when they saw me. And they were not able to behold me because of the majestic glory and beauty of the appearance of the shining light of the crown of glory upon my head.

CHAPTER 15

Metatron transformed into fire

R. Ishmael said: Metatron, the angel, the Prince of the Presence, the Glory of all heavens, said to me:

(1) As soon as the Holy One, blessed be He, took me in (His) service to attend the Throne of Glory and the Wheels (*Galgallim*) of the *Merkaba* and the needs of *Shekina*, forthwith my flesh was changed into flames, my sinews into flaming fire, my bones into coals of burning juniper, the light of my eyelids into splendor of lightnings, my eyeballs into firebrands, the hair of my head into dot flames, all my limbs into wings of burning fire and the whole of my body into glowing fire.

(2) And on my right were divisions of fiery flames, on my left firebrands were burning, round about me storm-wind and tempest were blowing and in front of me and behind me was roaring of thunder with earthquake.

CHAPTER 15-B

Addition occurring in B and L

B:

(1) *R. Ishmael said: Said to me*

Metatron, the Prince of the Presence and the prince over all the princes and he stands

L:

(1) *Metatron, he is prince over all the princes and he stands before*

before

Him who is greater than all the Elohim. And he goes in under the Throne of Glory. And he has a great tabernacle of light on high. And he brings forth the fire of deafness and puts (it) into the ears of the Holy Chayyoth, that they may not hear the voice of the Word (Dibbur) that goes forth from the mouth of the Divine Majesty.

(2)And when Moses ascended on high, he fasted 121 fasts, till the habitations of the chashmal were opened to him; and he

B:	L:
saw the heart within the heart of the Lion	*saw, that it was white as the heart of the Lion*

and he saw the innumerable companies of the hosts Around about him. And they desired to burn him. But Moses prayed for mercy, first for Israel and after that for himself: and He who sitteth on the Merkaba opened the windows that are above the heads of the Kerubim. And a host of 1800 advocates —and the Prince of the Presence, Metatron, with them—went forth to meet Moses. And they took the prayers of Israel and put them as a crown on the head of the Holy One, blessed be He.

(3)And they said (Deut. 6:4): "Hear, O Israel; the Lord our God is one Lord"

B:	L:
and their face shone and rejoiced over Shekina	*and the face of Shekina shone and rejoiced*

and they said to Metatron: "What are these? And to whom do they give all this honor and glory?" And they answered: "To the Glorious Lord of Israel". And they spake:

B:	L:
"Hear, O Israel: the Lord, our God, is one Lord. To whom shall be given abundance of honor and majesty but to Thee YHWH, the Divine Majesty, the King, living and eternal".	*"YHWH the Living and Eternal".*

(4)In that moment spake Akatriel Yah Yehod Sebaoth and said to Metatron, the Prince of the Presence: "Let no prayer that he prayeth before me return (to him) void. Hear thou his prayer and fulfill his desire whether (it be) great or small".

(5)Forthwith Metatron, the Prince of the Presence, said to Moses: "Son of Amram! Fear not, for now God delights in thee. And ask thou thy desire of the Glory and Majesty. For thy face shines from one end of the world to the other". But Moses answered him: "(I fear) lest I

bring guiltiness upon myself". *Metatron said to him: "Receive the letters of the oath, in (by) which there is no breaking the covenant"* (which precludes any breach of the covenant).

CHAPTER 16

Probably additional

Metatron divested of his privilege of presiding on a Throne of his own on account of Acker's misapprehension in taking him for a second Divine Power

R. Ishmael said: Metatron, the Angel, the Prince of the Presence, the Glory of all heaven, said to me:

[1]At first I was sitting upon a great Throne at the door of the Seventh Hall; and I was judging the children of heaven, the household on high by authority of the Holy One, blessed be He. And I divided Greatness, Kingship, Dignity, Rulership, Honor and Praise, and Diadem and Crown of Glory unto all the princes of kingdoms, while I was presiding (lit. sitting) in the Celestial Court (*Yeshiba*), and the princes of kingdoms were standing before me, on my right and on my left by authority of the Holy One, blessed be He.

[2]But when Acher came to behold the vision of the *Merkaba* and fixed his eyes on me, he feared and trembled before me and his soul was affrighted even unto departing from him, because of fear, horror and dread of me, when he beheld me sitting upon a throne like a king with all the ministering angels standing by me as my servants and all the princes of kingdoms adorned with crowns surrounding me: [3]in that moment he opened his mouth and said: "Indeed, there are two Divine Powers in heaven!" [4]Forthwith *Bath Qol* (the Divine Voice) went forth from heaven from before the *Shekina* and said: "Return, ye backsliding children (Jer. 3:22), except Acher!"

[5]Then came '*Aniyel*, the Prince, the honored, glorified, beloved, wonderful, revered and fearful one, in commission from the Holy One, blessed be He and gave me sixty strokes with lashes of fire and made me stand on my feet.

CHAPTER 17

*The princes of the seven heavens, of the sun, moon, planets
and constellations and their suites of angels*

R. Ishmael said: Metatron, the angel, the Prince of the Presence, the glory of all heavens, said to me:

(1)Seven (are the) princes, the great, beautiful, revered, wonderful and honored ones who are appointed over the seven heavens. And these are they:

A:

MIKAEL, GABRIEL, SHATQIEL, SHACHAQIEL, BAKARIEL, BADARIEL, PACHRIEL.

D:

MIKAEL and GABRIEL, SHATQIEL and BARADIEL and SHACHAQIEL and BARAQIEL and SIDRIEL.

(2)And every one of them is the prince of the host of (one) heaven. And each one of them is accompanied by 496,000 myriads of ministering angels.

(3)MIKAEL, the great prince, is appointed over the seventh heaven, the highest one, which is in the *'Araboth*.

GABRIEL, the prince of the host, is appointed over the sixth heaven which is in *Makon*.

SHATAQIEL, prince of the host, is appointed over the fifth heaven which is in *Ma'on*.

SHAHAQI'EL, prince of the host, is appointed over the fourth heaven which is in *Zebul*.

BADARIEL, prince of the host, is appointed over the third heaven which is in *Shehaqim*.

BARAKIEL, prince of the host, is appointed over the second heaven which is in the height of (Merom) *Raqia*.

PAZRIEL, prince of the host, is appointed over the first heaven which is in Wilon, which is in *Shamayim*.

(4)Under them is GALGALLIEL, the prince who is appointed over the globe (*galgal*) of the sun, and with him are 96 great and honored angels who move the sun in *Raqia*.

(5)Under them is 'OPHANNIEL, the prince who is set over the globe (*'ophan*) of the moon. And with him are 88 angels who move the globe of the moon 354 thousand parasangs every night at the time when the moon stands in the East at its turning point.

And when is the moon sitting in the East at its turning point? Answer: in the fifteenth day of every month.

[6]Under them is RAHATIEL, the prince who is appointed over the constellations. And he is accompanied by 72 great and honored angels. And why is he called RAHATIEL? Because he makes the stars run (*marhit*) in their orbits and courses 339 thousand parasangs every night from the East to the West, and from the West to the East. For the Holy One, blessed be He, has made a tent for all of them, for the sun, the moon, the planets and the stars in which they travel at night from the West to the East.

[7]Under them is KOKBIEL, the prince who is appointed over all the planets. And with him are 365,000 myriads of ministering angels, great and honored ones who move the planets from city to city and from province to province in the *Raqia* of heavens.

[8]And over them are SEVENTY-TWO PRINCES OF KINGDOMS on high corresponding to the 72 tongues of the world. And all of them are crowned with royal crowns and clad in royal garments and wrapped in royal cloaks. And all of them are riding on royal horses and they are holding royal scepters in their hands. And before each one of them when he is traveling in *Raqia*, royal servants are running with great glory and majesty

A:

even as on earth they (princes) are traveling in chariot(s) with horsemen and great armies and in glory and greatness with praise, song and honor.

D:

and before every one of them, when traveling in *Raqia'*, there are running great armies, even as (the custom is) on earth, with chariot(s), in glory and greatness, praise, song and honor,

CHAPTER 18

The order of ranks of the angels and the homage received by the higher ranks from the lower ones

R. Ishmael said: Metatron, the Angel, the Prince of the Presence, the glory of all heaven, said to me:

[1]THE ANGELS OF THE FIRST HEAVEN, when(ever) they see their prince, they dismount from their horses and fall on their faces. And THE PRINCE OF THE

FIRST HEAVEN, when he sees the prince of the second heaven, he dismounts, removes the *crown of glory* from his head and falls on his face.

And THE PRINCE OF THE SECOND HEAVEN, when he sees the prince of the third heaven, he removes the crown of glory from his head and falls on his face.

And THE PRINCE OF THE THIRD HEAVEN, when he sees the prince of the fourth heaven, he removes the crown of glory from his head and falls on his face.

And THE PRINCE OF THE FOURTH HEAVEN, when he sees the prince of the fifth heaven, he removes the crown of glory from his head and falls on his face.

And THE PRINCE OF THE FIFTH HEAVEN, when he sees the prince of the sixth heaven, he removes the crown of glory from his head and falls on his face.

And THE PRINCE OF THE SIXTH HEAVEN, when he sees the prince of the seventh heaven, he removes the crown of glory from his head and falls on his face.

[2] And THE PRINCE OF THE SEVENTH HEAVEN, when he sees THE SEVENTY-TWO PRINCES OF KINGDOMS, he removes the crown of glory from his head and falls on his face.

[3] And the seventy-two princes of kingdoms, when they see THE DOOR KEEPERS OF THE FIRST HALL IN THE 'ARABOTH RAQIA in the highest, they remove the royal crown from their head and fall on their faces.

And THE DOOR KEEPERS OF THE FIRST HALL, when they see the doorkeepers of the second Hall, they remove the crown of glory from their head and fall on their faces.

And THE DOOR KEEPERS OF THE SECOND HALL, when they see the doorkeepers of the third Hall, they remove the crown of glory from their head and fall on their faces.

And THE DOOR KEEPERS OF THE THIRD HALL, when they see the doorkeepers of the fourth Hall, they remove the crown of glory from their head and fall on their faces.

And THE DOOR KEEPERS OF THE FOURTH HALL, when they see the doorkeepers of the fifth Hall, they remove the crown of glory from their head and fall on their faces.

And THE DOOR KEEPERS OF THE FIFTH HALL, when they see the doorkeepers of the sixth Hall, they remove the crown of glory from their head and fall on their faces.

And THE DOOR KEEPERS OF THE SIXTH HALL, when they see the DOOR KEEPERS OF THE SEVENTH HALL, they remove the crown of glory from their head and fall on their faces.

(4)And the door keepers of the seventh Hall, when they see THE FOUR GREAT PRINCES, the honored ones, WHO ARE APPOINTED OVER THE FOUR CAMPS OF SHEKINA, they remove the crown(s) of glory from their head and fall on their faces.

(5)And the four great princes, when they see TAG'AS, the prince, great and honored with song (and) praise, at the head of all the children of heaven, they remove the crown of glory from their head and fall on their faces.

(6)And Tag'as, the great and honored prince, when he sees BARATTIEL, the great prince of three fingers in the height of 'Araboth, the highest heaven, he removes the crown of glory from his head and falls on his face.

(7)And Barattiel, the great prince, when he sees HAMON, the great prince, the fearful and honored, pleasant and terrible one who maketh all the children of heaven to tremble, when the time draweth nigh (that is set) for the saying of the '(Thrice) Holy', as it is written (Isa. 33:3): "At the noise of the tumult (hamon) the peoples are fled; at the lifting up of thyself the nations are scattered" he removes the crown of glory from his head and falls on his face.

(8)And Hamon, the great prince, when he sees TUTRESIEL, the great prince, he removes the crown of glory from his head and falls on his face.

(9)And Tutresiel H', the great prince, when he sees ATRUGIEL, the great prince, he removes the crown of glory from his head and falls on his face.

(10)And Atrugiel the great prince, when he sees NA'ARIRIEL H', the great prince, he removes the crown of glory from his head and falls on his face.

(11)And Na'aririel H', the great prince, when he sees SASNIGIEL, the great prince, he removes the crown of glory from his head and falls on his face.

(12)And Sasnigiel H', when he sees ZAZRIEL H', the great prince, he removes the crown of glory from his head and falls on his face.

(13)And Zazriel H', the prince, when he sees GEBURATIEL H', the prince, he removes the crown of glory from his head and falls on his face.

(14)And Geburatiel H', the prince, when he sees 'ARAPHIEL H', the prince, he removes the crown of glory from his head and falls on his face.

(15) And 'Araphiel H', the prince, when he secs 'ASHRUYLU, the prince, who presides in all the sessions of the children of heaven, he removes the crown of glory from his head and falls on his face.

(16) And Ashruylu H, the prince, when he sees GALLISUR H', THE PRINCE, WHO REVEALS ALL THE SECRETS OF THE LAW (Tora), he removes the crown of glory from his head and falls on his face.

(17) And Gallisur H', the prince, when he sees ZAKZAKIEL H', the prince who is appointed to write down the merits of Israel on the Throne of Glory, he removes the crown of glory from his head and falls on his face.

(18) And Zakzakiel H', the great prince, when he sees 'ANAPH(I)EL H', the prince who keeps the keys of the heavenly Halls, he removes the crown of glory from his head and falls on his face. Why is he called by the name of 'Anaphiel? Because the bough of his honor and majesty and his crown and his splendor and his brilliance covers (overshadows) all the chambers of 'Araboth Raqia on high even as the Maker of the World (doth overshadow them). Just as it is written with regard to the Maker of the World (Hab. 3:3): "His glory covered the heavens, and the earth was full of his praise", even so do the honor and majesty of 'Anaphiel cover all the glories of 'Araboth the highest.

(19) And when he sees SOTHER 'ASHIEL H', the prince, the great, fearful and honored one, he removes the crown of glory from his head and falls on his face. Why is he called Sother Ashiel? Because he is appointed over the four heads of the fiery river over against the Throne of Glory; and every single prince who goes out or enters before the *Shekina*, goes out or enters only by his permission. For the seals of the fiery river are entrusted to him. And furthermore, his height is 7000 myriads of parasangs. And he stirs up the fire of the river; and he goes out and enters before the *Shekina* to expound what is written (recorded) concerning the inhabitants of the world. According as it is written (Dan. 7:10):" the judgment was set, and the books were opened".

(20) And Sother 'Ashiel the prince, when he sees SHOQED CHOZI, the great prince, the mighty, terrible and honored one, he removes the crown of glory from his head and falls upon his face. And why is he called Shoqed Chozi? Because he weighs all the merits (of man) in a balance in the presence of the Holy One, blessed be He.

(21) And when he sees ZEHANPURYU H', the great prince, the mighty and terrible one, honored, glorified and feared in all the heavenly household, he removes the crown of glory from his head and falls on his face. Why is he called Zehanpuryu? Because he rebukes the fiery river and pushes it back to its place.

(22) And when he sees 'AZBUGA H', the great prince, glorified, revered, honored, adorned, wonderful, exalted, beloved and feared among all the great princes who know

the mystery of the Throne of Glory, he removes the crown of glory from his head and falls on his face. Why is he called 'Azbuga? Because in the future he will gird (clothe) the righteous and pious of the world with the garments of life and wrap them in the cloak of life, that they may live in them an eternal life.

(23)And when he sees the two great princes, the strong and glorified ones who are standing above him, he removes the crown of glory from his head and falls on his face. And these are the names of the two princes:

SOPHERIEL H' (WHO) KILLETH, (Sopheriel H' the Killer), the great prince, the honored, glorified, blameless, venerable, ancient and mighty one; (and) SOPHERIEL H' (WHO) MAKETH ALIVE (Sopheriel H' the Lifegiver), the great prince, the honored, glorified, blameless, ancient and mighty one.

(24)Why is he called Sopheriel H' who killeth (Sopheriel H' the Killer)? Because he is appointed over the books of the dead: [so that] everyone, when the day of his death draws nigh, he writes him in the books of the dead.

Why is he called Sopheriel H' who maketh alive (Sopheriel H' the Lifegiver)? Because he is appointed over the books of the living (of life), so that everyone whom the Holy One, blessed be He, will bring into life, he writes him in the book of the living (of life), by authority of MAQOM. Thou might perhaps say: "Since the Holy One, blessed be He, is sitting on a throne, they also are sitting when writing". (Answer): The Scripture teaches us (Kings 22:19, 2 Chron. 18:18): "And all the host of heaven are standing by him ".

"The host of heaven" (it is said) in order to show us, that even the Great Princes, none like whom there is in the high heavens, do not fulfill the requests of the *Shekina* otherwise than standing. But how is it (possible that) they (are able to) write, when they are standing?

It is like this:

(25)One is standing on the wheels of the tempest and the other is standing on the wheels of the storm-wind.

The one is clad in kingly garments, the other is clad in kingly garments.

The one is wrapped in a mantle of majesty and the other is wrapped in a mantle of majesty.

The one is crowned with a royal crown, and the other is crowned with a royal crown.

The one's body is full of eyes, and the other's body is full of eyes.

The appearance of one is like unto the appearance of lightnings, and the appearance of the other is like unto the appearance of lightnings.

The eyes of the one are like the sun in its might, and the eyes of the other are like the sun in its might.

The one's height is like the height of the seven heavens, and the other's height is like the height of the seven heavens.

The wings of the one are as (many as) the days of the year, and the wings of the other are as (many as) the days of the year.

The wings of the one extend over the breadth of *Raqia*, and the wings of the other extend over the breadth of *Raqia*.

The lips of the one, are as the gates of the East, and the lips of the other are as the gates of the East.

The tongue of the one is as high as the waves of the sea, and the tongue of the other is as high as the waves of the sea.

From the mouth of the one a flame goes forth, and from the mouth of the other a flame goes forth.

From the mouth of the one there go forth lightnings and from the mouth of the other there go forth lightnings.

From the sweat of the one fire is kindled, and from the perspiration of the other fire is kindled.

From the one's tongue a torch is burning, and from the tongue of the other a torch is burning.

On the head of the one there is a sapphire stone, and upon the head of the other there is a sapphire stone.

On the shoulders of the one there is a wheel of a swift cherub, and on the shoulders of the other there is a wheel of a swift cherub.

One has in his hand a burning scroll, the other has in his hand a burning scroll.

The one has in his hand a flaming style, the other has in his hand a flaming style.

The length of the scroll is 3000 myriads of parasangs; the size of the style is 3000 myriads of parasangs; the size of every single letter that they write is 365 parasangs.

CHAPTER 19

*Rikbiel, the prince of the wheels of the Merkaba. The
surroundings of the Merkaba. The commotion among the
angelic hosts at the time of the Qedushsha*

R. Ishmael said: Metatron, the Angel, the Prince of the Presence, said to me:

[1] Above these three angels, these great princes there is one Prince, distinguished, honored, noble, glorified, adorned, fearful, valiant, strong, great, magnified, glorious, crowned, wonderful, exalted, blameless, beloved, lordly, high and lofty, ancient and mighty, like unto whom there is none among the princes. His name is RIKBIEL H', the great and revered prince who is standing by the *Merkaba*.

[2] And why is he called RIKBIEL? Because he is appointed over the wheels of the *Merkaba*, and they are given in his charge. [3] And how many are the wheels? Eight; two in each direction. And there are four winds compassing them round about. And these are their names: "the Storm-Wind", "the Tempest", "the Strong Wind", and "the Wind of Earthquake". [4] And under them four fiery rivers are continually running, one fiery river on each side. And round about them, between the rivers, four clouds are planted (placed), and these they are: "clouds of fire", "clouds of lamps", "clouds of coal", "clouds of brimstone" and they are standing over against [their] wheels.

[5] And the feet of the *Chayyoth* are resting upon the wheels. And between one wheel and the other earthquake is roaring and thunder is thundering.

[6] And when the time draws nigh for the recital of the Song, (then) the multitudes of wheels are moved, the multitude of clouds tremble, all the chieftains (*shallishim*) are made afraid, all the horsemen (*parashim*) do rage, all the mighty ones (*gibborim*) are excited, all the hosts (*seba'im*) are affrighted, all the troops (*gedudim*) are in fear, all the appointed ones (*memunnim*) haste away, all the princes (*sarim*) and armies (*chayyelim*) are dismayed, all the servants (*mesharetim*) do faint and all the angels (*mal'akim*) and divisions (*degalim*) travail with pain.

[7] And one wheel makes a sound to be heard to the other and one *Kerub* to another, one *Chayya*. to another, one *Seraph* to another (saying) (Ps. 17:5) "Extol to him that rideth in 'Araboth, by his name *Jah* and rejoice before him!"

CHAPTER 20

CHAYYLIEL, the prince of the Chayyoth

R. Ishmael said: Metatron, the angel, the Prince of the Presence, said to me:

(1)Above these there is one great and mighty prince. His name is *CHAYYLIEL H'*, a noble and revered prince, a glorious and mighty prince, a great and revered prince, a prince before whom all the children of heaven do tremble, a prince who is able to swallow up the whole earth in one moment (at a mouthful).

(2)And why is he called *CHAYYLIEL H'*? Because he is appointed over the *Holy Chayyoth* and smites the *Chayyoth* with lashes of fire: and glorifies them, when they give praise and glory and rejoicing and he causes them to make haste to say "Holy" and "Blessed be the Glory of *H'* from his place!" (i.e. the *Qedushsha*).

CHAPTER 21

The Chayyoth

R. Ishmael said: Metatron, the angel, the Prince of the Presence, said to me:

(1)Four (are) the *Chayyoth* corresponding to the four winds. Each *Chayya* is as the space of the whole world. And each one has four faces; and each face is as the face of the East. (2)Each one has four wings and each wing is like the cover (roof) of the universe. (3)And each one has faces in the middle of faces and wings in the middle of wings. The size of the faces is (as the size of) 248 faces, and the size of the wings is (as the size of) 365 wings.

(4)And everyone is crowned with 2000 crowns on his head. And each crown is like unto the bow in the cloud. And its splendor is like unto the splendor of the globe of the sun. And the sparks that go forth from everyone are like the splendor of the morning star (planet Venus) in the East.

CHAPTER 22

KERUBIEL, the Prince of the Kerubim;
Description of the Kerubim

R. Ishmael said: Metatron, the angel, the Prince of the Presence, said to me:

[1] Above these there is one prince, noble, wonderful, strong, and praised with all kinds of praise. His name is KERUBIEL *H'*, a mighty prince, full of power and strength

AD:	*B:*
a prince of highness, and Highness (is) with him, a righteous prince, and righteousness (is) with him, a holy prince, and holiness (is) with him, a prince	a prince of highness, and with him (there is) a righteous prince, of righteousness, and with him a holy prince, of holiness, and with him (there is) a prince

glorified in (by) thousand hosts, exalted by ten thousand armies.

[2] At his wrath the earth trembles, at his anger the camps are moved, from fear of him the foundations are shaken, at his rebuke the *'Araboth* do tremble.

[3] His stature is full of (burning) coals. The height of his stature is as the height of the seven heavens the breadth of his stature is as the wideness of the seven heavens and the thickness of his stature is as the seven heavens.

[4] The opening of his mouth is like a lamp of fire. His tongue is a consuming fire. His eyebrows are like unto the splendor of the lightning. His eyes are like sparks of brilliance. His countenance is like a burning fire.

[5] And there is a crown of holiness upon his head on which (crown) the Explicit Name is graven, and lightnings go forth from it. And the bow of *Shekina* is between his shoulders.

[6] | *AD:* | *B:* |
|---|---|
| And his sword is upon his loins and his arrows are like lightnings in his girdle. And a shield of consuming fire (is) on his neck and coals of juniper are round about him. | And his sword is like unto a lightning; and upon his loins there are arrows like unto a flame, and upon his armor and shield there is a consuming fire, and upon his neck there are coals of burning juniper and (also) round about him (there are coals of burning juniper). |

[7] And the splendor of *Shekina* is on his face; and the horns of majesty on his wheels; and a royal diadem upon his skull.

[8] And his body is full of eyes. And wings are covering the whole of his high stature (lit. the height of his stature is all wings).

(9)On his right hand a flame is burning, and on his left a fire is glowing; and coals are burning from it. And firebrands go forth from his body. And lightnings are cast forth from his face. With him there is always thunder upon (in) thunder, by his side there is ever earthquake upon (in) earthquake.

(10)And the two princes of the *Merkaba* are together with him.

(11)Why is he called KERUBIEL *H'*, the Prince. Because he is appointed over the chariot of the *Kerubim*. And the mighty *Kerubim* are given in his charge. And he adorns the crowns on their heads and polishes the diadem upon their skull.

(12)He magnifies the glory of their appearance. And he glorifies the beauty of their majesty. And he increases the greatness of their honor. He causes the song of their praise to be sung. He intensifies their beautiful strength. He causes the brilliance of their glory to shine forth. He beautifies their goodly mercy and loving-kindness. He frames the fairness of their radiance. He makes their merciful beauty even more beautiful. He glorifies their upright majesty. He extols the order of their praise, to stablish the dwelling place of him "who dwelleth on the *Kerubim*".

(13)And the *Kerubim* are standing by the Holy *Chayyoth*, and their wings are raised up to their heads (lit. are as the height of their heads)

> and *Shekina* is (resting) upon them
> and the brilliance of the Glory is upon their faces
> and song and praise in their mouth
> and their hands are under their wings
> and their feet are covered by their wings
> and horns of glory are upon their heads
> and the splendor of *Shekina* on their face
> and *Shekina* is (resting) upon them
> and sapphire stones are round about them
> and columns of fire on their four sides
> and columns of firebrands beside them.

(14)There is one sapphire on one side and another sapphire on another side and under the sapphires there are coals of burning juniper.

(15)And one *Kerub* is standing in each direction but the wings of the *Kerubim* compass each other above their skulls in glory; and they spread them to sing with them a song to him that inhabiteth the clouds and to praise with them the fearful majesty of the king of kings.

(16)And KERUBIEL *H'*, the prince who is appointed over them, he arrays them in comely, beautiful and pleasant orders and he exalts them in all manner of exaltation, dignity and glory. And he hastens them in glory and might to do the will of their

Creator every moment. For above their lofty heads abides continually the glory of the high king "who dwelleth on the *Kerubim*".

<h1 style="text-align:center">CHAPTER 22-B</h1>

L(mr), following after the rec. of ch. 22 c. vss. 1-3 (middle):

B:

R. Ishmael said to me: Metatron, the angel, the Prince of the Presence, said to me:

[1]*And there is a court before the Throne of Glory,*

[1]*How are the angels standing on high? He said: Like a bridge that is placed over a river so that everyone can pass over it, likewise a bridge is placed from the beginning of the entry to the end.* [2]*And three ministering angels surround it and utter a song before YHWH, the God of Israel. And there are standing before it lords of dread and captains of fear, thousand times thousand and ten thousand times ten thousand in number and they sing praise and hymns before YHWH, the God of Israel.*

[2]*which no seraph nor angel can enter, and it is 36,000 myriads of parasangs, as it is written (Is. 6:2): "and the Seraphim are standing above him" (the last word of the scriptural passage being ' לו ' [numerical value: 36]).*

[3]*Numerous bridges are there: bridges of fire and numerous bridges of hail. Also numerous rivers of hail, numerous treasuries of snow and numerous wheels of fire.*

[3]*As the numerical value* לו *(36) is the number of the bridges there.*

[4]*And there are 24 myriads of wheels of fire. And the ministering angels are 12,000 myriads. And there are 12,000 rivers of hail, and 12,000 treasuries of snow. And in the seven Halls are chariots of fire and flames,*

[4]*And how many are the ministering angels? 12,000 myriads: six (thousand myriads) above and six (thousand myriads) below. And 12,000 are the treasuries of snow, six above and six below. And 24 myriads of*

without reckoning, or end or searching. (Lmr. ends here.)

wheels of fire, 12 (myriads] above and 12 (myriads) below. And they surround the bridges and the rivers of fire and the rivers of hail. And there are numerous ministering angels, forming entries, for all

the creatures that are standing in the midst thereof, corresponding to (over against) the paths of Raqia Shamayim.

(5)*What doeth YHWH, the God of Israel, the King of Glory? The Great and Fearful God, mighty in strength, doth cover his face.*

(6)*In Araboth are 660,000 myriads of angels of glory standing over against the Throne of Glory and the divisions of flaming fire. And the King of Glory doth cover His face; for else the (Araboth Raqia would be rent asunder in its midst because of the majesty, splendor, beauty, radiance, loveliness, brilliancy, brightness and excellency of the appearance of (the Holy One,) blessed be He.*

(7)*There are numerous ministering angels performing his will, numerous kings, numerous princes in the 'Araboth of his delight, angels who are revered among the rulers in heaven, distinguished, adorned with song and bringing love to remembrance: (who) are affrighted by the splendor of the Shekina, and their eyes are dazzled by the shining beauty of their King, their faces grow black and their strength doth fail.*

(8)*There go forth rivers of joy, streams of gladness, rivers of rejoicing, streams of triumph, rivers of love, streams of friendship (another reading:) of commotion and they flow over and go forth before the Throne of Glory and wax great and go through the gates of the paths of 'Araboth Raqia at the voice of the shouting and music of the CHAYYOTH, at the voice of the rejoicing of the timbrels of his 'OPHANNIM and at the melody of the cymbals of His Kerubim. And they wax great and go forth with commotion with the sound of the hymn: "HOLY, HOLY, HOLY, IS THE LORD OF HOSTS; THE WHOLE EARTH IS FULL OF HIS GLORY!"*

CHAPTER 22-C

(in B, Lo and Lmr)

R. Ishmael said: Metatron, the Prince of the Presence said to me:

(1)*What is the distance between one bridge and another? 12 myriads of parasangs. Their ascent is 12 myriads of parasangs, and their descent 12 myriads of parasangs.*

(2)*(The distance) between the rivers of dread and the rivers of fear is 22 myriads of parasangs; between the rivers of hail and the rivers of darkness 36 myriads of parasangs; between the chambers of lightnings and the clouds of compassion 42 myriads of parasangs; between the clouds of compassion and the Merkaba 84 myriads of parasangs; between the Merkaba and the Kerubim 148 myriads of parasangs; between the Kerubim and the 'Ophannim 24 myriads of parasangs; between the Ophannim and the chambers of chambers 24 myriads of parasangs; between the chambers of chambers and the Holy Chayyoth 40,000 myriads of parasangs; between one wing (of the Chayyoth) and another 12 myriads of parasangs; and the breadth of each one wing is of that same measure; and the distance between the Holy Chayyoth and the Throne of Glory is 30,000 myriads of parasangs.*

(3)*And from the foot of the Throne to the seat there are 40,000 myriads of parasangs. And the name of Him that sitteth on it: let the name be sanctified!*

[(4)*And the arches of the Bow are set above the 'Araboth, and they are 1000 thousands and 10,000 times ten thousands (of parasangs) high. Their measure is after the measure of the 'Irin and Qaddishin (Watchers and Holy Ones). As it is written (Gen. 9:13) "My bow I have set in the cloud". It is not written here "I will set" but "I have set", (i.e.) already; clouds that surround the Throne of Glory. As His clouds pass by, the angels of hail (turn into) burning coal.*

(5)*And a fire of the voice goes down from by the Holy Chayyoth. And because of the breath of that voice they "run" (Ezek. 1:14) to another place, fearing lest it command them to go; and they "return" lest it injure them from the other side. Therefore "they run and return" (Ezek. 1:14).*

(6)*And these arches of the Bow are more beautiful and radiant than the radiance of the sun during the summer solstice. And they are whiter than a flaming fire and they are great and beautiful.*

(7)*Above the arches of the Bow are the wheels of the 'Ophannim. Their height is 1000 thousand and 10,000 times 10,000 units of measure after the measure of the Seraphim and the Troops (Gedudim).*]

CHAPTER 23

The winds blowing 'under the wings of the Kerubim'

R. Ishmael said: Metatron, the Angel, the Prince of the Presence, said to me:

(1)There are numerous winds blowing under the wings of the *Kerubim*.

There blows "the Brooding Wind", as it is written (Gen. 1:2): "and the wind of God was brooding upon the face of the waters ".

(2)There blows "the Strong Wind", as it is said (Ex. 14:21): "and the Lord caused the sea to go back by a strong east wind all that night".

(3)There blows "the East Wind" as it is written (Ex. 10:13): "the east wind brought the locusts".

(4)There blows "the Wind of Quails" as it is written (Num. 11:31): "And there went forth a wind from the Lord and brought quails ".

(5)There blows "the Wind of Jealousy" as it is written (Num. 5:14): "And the wind of jealousy came upon him".

(6)There blows the "Wind of Earthquake" as it is written (1 Kings 19:11): "and after that the wind of the earthquake; but the Lord was not in the earthquake".

(7)There blows the "Wind of *H'* " 3 as it is written (Ex. 37:1): "and he carried me out by the wind of *H'* and set me down ".

(8)There blows the "Evil Wind" as it is written (1 Sam. 16:23): "and the evil wind departed from him".

(9)There blow the "Wind of Wisdom" and the "Wind of Understanding" and the "Wind of Knowledge" and the "Wind of the Fear of *H'*" as it is written (Is. 11:2): "And the wind of *H'* shall rest upon him; the wind of wisdom and understanding, the wind of counsel and might, the wind of knowledge and of the fear of *H'*".

(10)There blows the "Wind of Rain", as it is written (Prov. 25:23): "the north wind bringeth forth rain".

(11)There blows the "Wind of Lightnings ", as it is written (Jer. 10:13, 51:16): "he maketh lightnings for the rain and bringeth forth the wind out of his treasuries ".

(12)There blows the "Wind, Breaking the Rocks", as it is written (1 Kings 19:11): "the Lord passed by and a great and strong wind (rent the mountains and brake in pieces the rocks before the Lord)".

(13)There blows the "Wind of Assuagement of the Sea", as it is written (Gen. 8:1): "and God made a wind to pass over the earth, and the waters assuaged".

(14)There blows the "Wind of Wrath", as it is written (Job 1:19): "and behold there came a great wind from the wilderness and smote the four corners of the house and it fell".

(15)There blows the "Storm-Wind", as it is written (Ps. 148:8): "Storm-wind, fulfilling his word".

(16)And Satan is standing among these winds, for "storm-wind" is nothing else but "Satan", and all these winds do not blow but under the wings of the *Kerubim*, as it is written (Ps. 18:11): "and he rode upon a cherub and did fly, yea, and he flew swiftly upon the wings of the wind".

(17)And whither go all these winds? The Scripture teaches us, that they go out from under the wings of the *Kerubim* and descend on the globe of the sun, as it is written (Eccl. 1:6): "The wind goeth toward the south and turneth about unto the north; it turneth about continually in its course and the wind returneth again to its circuits ". And from the globe of the sun they return and descend upon [the rivers and the seas, upon] the mountains and upon the hills, as it is written (Am. 4:13): "For lo, he that formeth the mountains and createth the wind".

(18)And from the mountains and the hills they return and descend to the seas and the rivers; and from the seas and the rivers they return and descend upon (the) cities and provinces; and from the cities and provinces they return and descend into the Garden, and from the Garden they return and descend to Eden, as it is written (Gen. 3:8): "walking in the Garden in the wind of day". And in the midst of the Garden they join together and blow from one side to the other and are perfumed with the spices of the Garden even from its remotest parts, until they separate from each other, and, filled with the scent of the pure spices, they bring the odor from the remotest parts of Eden and the spices of the Garden to the righteous and godly who in the time to come shall inherit the Garden of Eden and the Tree of Life, as it is written (Cant. 4:16): "Awake, O north wind; and come thou south; blow upon my garden, that the spices thereof may flow out. Let my beloved come into his garden and eat his precious fruits".

CHAPTER 24

The different chariots of the Holy One, blessed be He

R. Ishmael said: Metatron, the Angel, the Prince of the Presence, the glory of all heaven, said to me:

(1)Numerous chariots has the Holy One, blessed be He:

He has the "Chariots of (the) *Kerubim*", as it is written (Ps. 18:11, 2 Sam. 22:11): "And he rode upon a cherub and did fly".

(2)He has the "Chariots of Wind", as it is written (ib.): "and he flew swiftly upon the wings of the wind ".

(3)He has the "Chariots of (the) Swift Cloud", as it is written (Is. 19:1): "Behold, the Lord rideth upon a swift cloud".

(4)He has "the Chariots of Clouds", as it is written (Ex. 19:9): "Lo, I come unto thee in a cloud".

(5)He has the "Chariots of the Altar", as it is written (Am. 9:1): "I saw the Lord standing upon the Altar".

(6)He has the "Chariots of *Ribbotaim*", as it is written (Ps. 17:18): "The chariots of God are *Ribbotaim*; thousands of angels ".

(7)He has the "Chariots of the Tent", as it is written (Deut. 31:15): "And the Lord appeared in the Tent in a pillar of cloud ".

(8)He has the "Chariots of the Tabernacle", as it is written (Lev. 1:1): "And the Lord spake unto him out of the tabernacle".

(9)He has the "Chariots of the Mercy-Seat", as it is written (Num. 7:89): "then he heard the Voice speaking unto him from upon the mercy-seat".

(10)He has the "Chariots of Sapphire Stone", as it is written (Ex. 24:10): "and there was under his feet as it were a paved work of sapphire stone".

(11)He has the "Chariots of Eagles", as it is written (Ex. 19:4): "I bare you on eagles' wings". Eagles literally are not meant here but "they that fly swiftly as eagles".

(12)He has the "chariots of Shout", as it is written (Ps. 47:6):"God is gone up with a shout".

(13)He has the "Chariots of '*Araboth*'", as it is written (Ps. 17:5): "Extol Him that rideth upon the '*Araboth*'".

(14)He has the "Chariots of Thick Clouds", as it is written (Ps. 104:3): "who maketh the thick clouds His chariot".

(15)He has the "Chariots of the *Chayyoth*", as it is written (Ezek. 1:14): "and the *Chayyoth* ran and returned". They run by permission and return by permission, for *Shekina* is above their heads.

(16)He has the "Chariots of Wheels (Galgallim)", as it is written (Ezek. 10:2): "And he said: Go in between the whirling wheels".

(17)He has the "Chariots of a Swift *Kerub*", as it is written (?): "riding on a swift cherub". And at the time when He rides on a swift kerub, as he sets one of His feet upon him, before he sets the other foot upon his back, he looks through eighteen thousand 10 worlds at one glance. And he discerns and sees into them all and knows what is in all of them—and then he sets down the other foot upon him, according as it is written (Ezek. 48:35): "Round about eighteen thousand".

Whence do we know that He looks through every one of them every day? It is written (Ps. 14:2): "He looked down from heaven upon the children of men to see if there were any that did understand, that did seek after God".

(18)He has the "Chariots of the '*Ophannim*", as it is written (Ezek. 10:12): "and the '*Ophannim* were full of eyes round about".

(19)He has the "Chariots of His Holy Throne", as it is written (Ps. 47:8): "God sitteth upon his holy throne ".

(20)He has the "chariots of the Throne of *Yah*", as it is written (Ex. 17:16): "Because a hand is lifted up upon the Throne of Jah".

(21)He has the "Chariots of the Throne of Judgment", as it is written (Is. 5:16): "but the Lord of hosts shall be exalted in judgment".

(22)He has the "Chariots of the Throne of Glory ", as it is written (Jer. 17:12): "The Throne of Glory, set on high from the beginning, is the place of our sanctuary".

(23)He has the "Chariots of the High and Exalted Throne", as it is written (Is. 6:1): "I saw the Lord sitting upon the high and exalted throne".

CHAPTER 25

'Ophphanniel, the prince of the 'Ophannim.
Description of the 'Ophannim

R. Ishmael said: Metatron, the Angel, the Prince of the Presence, said to me:

(1)Above these there is one great prince, revered, high, lordly, fearful, ancient and strong. '*OPHPHANNIEL H'* is his name.

(2)He has sixteen faces, four faces on each side, (also) hundred wings on each side. And he has 8466 eyes, corresponding to the days of the year.

A:	*DE:*
2190—and some say 2116—on each side.	2191 (E: 2196) and sixteen on each side.

(3)And those two eyes of his face, in each one of them lightnings are flashing, and from each one of them firebrands are burning; and no creature is able to behold them: for anyone who looks at them is burnt instantly.

(4)His height is (as) the distance of 2500 years' journey. No eye can behold and no mouth can tell the mighty power of his strength save the King of kings, the Holy One, blessed be He, alone.

(5)Why is he called 'OPHPHANNIEL?

Because he is appointed over the 'Ophannim and the 'Ophannim are given in his charge. He stands every day and attends and beautifies them. And he exalts and orders their apartment (*DE:* runnings) and polishes their standing-place and makes bright their dwellings, makes their corners even and cleanses their seats. And he waits upon them early and late, by day and by night, to increase their beauty, to make great their dignity and to make them "diligent in praise of their Creator.

(6)And all the 'Ophannim are full of eyes, and they are all full of brightness; seventy two sapphire stones are fixed on their garments on their right side and seventy two sapphire stones are fixed on their garments on their left side.

(7)And four carbuncle stones are fixed on the crown of every single one, the splendor of which proceeds in the four directions of 'Araboth even as the splendor of the globe of the sun proceeds in all the directions of the universe. And why is it called Carbuncle (Bareqet)? Because its splendor is like the appearance of a lightning (*Baraq*). And tents of splendor, tents of brilliance, tents of brightness as of sapphire and carbuncle enclose them because of the shining appearance of their eyes.

CHAPTER 26

SERAPHIEL, the Prince of the Seraphim. Description of the Seraphim

R. Ishmael said: Metatron, the Angel, the Prince of the Presence, said to me:

(1)Above these there is one prince, wonderful, noble, great, honorable, mighty, terrible, a chief and leader and a swift scribe, glorified, honored and beloved.

(2)He is altogether filled with splendor, full of praise and shining; and he is wholly full of brilliance, of light and of beauty; and the whole of him is filled with goodliness and greatness.

(3)His countenance is altogether like (that of) angels, but his body is like an eagle's body.

(4)His splendor is like unto lightnings, his appearance like fire brands, his beauty like unto sparks, his honor like fiery coals, his majesty like *chashmals*, his radiance like the light of the planet Venus. The image of him is like unto the Greater Light. His height is as the seven heavens. The light from his eyebrows is like the sevenfold light.

(5)The sapphire stone upon his head is as great as the whole universe and like unto the splendor of the very heavens in radiance.

(6)His body is full of eyes like the stars of the sky, innumerable and unsearchable. Every eye is like the planet Venus. Yet, there are some of them like the Lesser Light and some of them like unto the Greater Light. From his ankles to his knees (they are) like unto stars of lightning, from his knees to his thighs like unto the planet Venus, from his thighs to his loins like unto the moon, from his loins to his neck like the sun, from his neck to his skull like unto the Light Imperishable. (Cf. Zeph. 3:5.)

(7)The crown on his head is like unto the splendor of the Throne of Glory. The measure of the crown is the distance of 502 years' journey. There is no kind of splendor, no kind of brilliance, no kind of radiance, no kind of light in the universe but is fixed on that crown.

(8)The name of that prince is SERAPHIEL *H*". And the crown on his head, its name is "the Prince of Peace". And why is he called by the name of SERAPHIEL *H*'? Because he is appointed over the *Seraphim*. And the flaming *Seraphim* are given in his charge. And he presides over them by day and by night and teaches them song, praise, proclamation of beauty, might and majesty; that they may proclaim the beauty of their King in all manner of Praise and Sanctification (*Qedushsha*).

(9)How many are the *Seraphim*"? Four, corresponding to the four winds of the world. And how many wings have they each one of them? Six, corresponding to the six days of Creation. And how many faces have they? Each one of them four faces.

(10)The measure of the *Seraphim* and the height of each one of them correspond to the height of the seven heavens. The size of each wing is like the measure of all *Raqia*. The size of each face is like that of the face of the East.

(11)And each one of them gives forth light like unto the splendor of the Throne of Glory: so that not even the Holy *Chayyoth*, the honored '*Ophannim*, nor the majestic *Kerubim* are able to behold it. For everyone who beholds it, his eyes are darkened because of its great splendor.

(12)Why are they called *Seraphim*? Because they burn (*saraph*) the writing tables of Satan: Every day Satan is sitting, together with SAMMAEL, the Prince of Rome, and with DUBBIEL, the Prince of Persia, and they write the iniquities of Israel on writing tables which they hand over to the *Seraphim*, in order that they may present them before the Holy One, blessed be He, so that He may destroy Israel from the world. But the *Seraphim* know from the secrets of the Holy One, blessed be He, that he desires not, that this people Israel should perish. What do the *Seraphim*? Every day do they receive (accept) them from the hand of Satan and burn them in the burning fire over against the high and exalted Throne in order that they may not come before the Holy One, blessed be He, at the time when he is sitting upon the Throne of Judgment, judging the whole world in truth.

CHAPTER 27

RADWERIEL, the keeper of the Book of Records

R. Ishmael said: Metatron, the Angel of *H'*, the Prince of the Presence, said to me:

(1) Above the *Seraphim* there is one prince, exalted above all the princes, wondrous more than all the servants. His name is RADWERIEL *H'* who is appointed over the treasuries of the books.

(2) He fetches forth the Case of Writings (with) the Book of Records in it, and brings it before the Holy One, blessed be He. And he breaks the seals of the case, opens it, takes out the books and delivers them before the Holy One, blessed be He. And the Holy One, blessed be He, receives them of his hand and gives them in his sight to the Scribes, that they may read them in the Great *Beth Din* in the height of 'Araboth Raqia', before the heavenly household.

(3) And why is he called RADWERIELS? Because out of every word that goes forth from his mouth an angel is created: and he stands in the songs (in the singing company) of the ministering angels and utters a song before the Holy One, blessed be He when the time draws nigh for the recitation of the (*Thrice*) *Holy*.

CHAPTER 28

The 'Irin and Qaddishin

R. Ishmael said: Metatron, the Angel, the Prince of the Presence, said to me:

(1) Above all these there are four great princes, *'Irin* and *Qaddishin* by name: high, honored, revered, beloved, wonderful and glorious ones, greater than all the children of heaven. There is none like unto them among all the celestial princes and none their equal among all the Servants. For each one of them is equal to all the rest together.

(2) And their dwelling is over against the Throne of Glory, and their standing place over against the Holy One, blessed be He, so that the brilliance of their dwelling is a

reflection of the brilliance of the Throne of Glory. And the splendor of their countenance is a reflection of the splendor of *Shekina*.

(3)And they are glorified by the glory of the Divine Majesty (Gebura) and praised by (through) the praise of *Shekina*.

(4)And not only that, but the Holy One, blessed be He, does nothing in his world without first consulting them, but after that he doeth it. As it is written (Dan. 4:17): "The sentence is by the decree of the *'Irin* and the demand by the word of the *Qaddishin*."

(5)The 'Irin are two and the *Qaddishin* are two. And how are they standing before the Holy One, blessed be He? It is to be understood, that one *'Ir* is standing on one side and the other *'Ir* on the other side, and one *Qaddish* is standing on one side and the other on the other side.

(6)And ever do they exalt the humble, and they abase to the ground those that are proud, and they exalt to the height those that are humble.

(7)And every day, as the Holy One, blessed be He, is sitting upon the Throne of Judgment and judges the whole world, and the Books of the Living and the Books of the Dead are opened before Him, then all the children of heaven are standing before him in fear, dread, awe and trembling. At that time, (when) the Holy One, blessed be He, is sitting upon the Throne of Judgment to execute judgment, his garment is white as snow, the hair on his head as pure wool and the whole of his cloak is like the shining light. And he is covered with righteousness all over as with a coat of mail.

(8)And those *'Irin* and *Qaddishin* are standing before him like court officers before the judge. And they raise and argue every case and close the case that comes before the Holy One, blessed be He, in judgment, according as it is written (Dan. 4:17): "The sentence is by the decree of the *'Irin* and the demand by the word of the *Qaddishin*"

(9)Some of them argue and others pass the sentence in the Great *Beth Din* in 'Araboth. Some of them make the requests from before the Divine Majesty and some close the cases before the Most High. Others finish by going down and (confirming =) executing the sentences on earth below. According as it is written (Dan. 4:13, 14): "Behold an *'Ir* and a *Qaddish* came down from heaven and cried aloud and said thus, Hew down the tree, and cut off his branches, shake off his leaves, and scatter his fruit: let the beasts get away from under it, and the fowls from his branches ".

(10)Why are they called *'Irin* and *Qaddishin*? By reason that they sanctify the body and the spirit with lashes of fire on the third day of the judgment, as it is written (Hos. 6:2): "After two days will he revive us: on the third he will raise us up, and we shall live before him."

CHAPTER 29

Description of a class of angels

R. Ishmael said: Metatron, the Angel, the Prince of the Presence, said to me:

[1]Each one of them has seventy names corresponding to the seventy tongues of the world. And all of them are (based) upon the name of the Holy One, blessed be He. And every several name is written with a flaming style upon the Fearful Crown (*Kether Nora*) which is on the head of the high and exalted King.

[2]And from each one of them there go forth sparks and lightnings. And each one of them is beset with horns of splendor round about. From each one lights are shining forth, and each one is surrounded by tents of brilliance so that not even the *Seraphim* and the *Chayyoth* who are greater than all the children of heaven are able to behold them.

CHAPTER 30

The 72 princes of Kingdoms and the Prince of the World officiating at the Great Sanhedrin in heaven

R. Ishmael said: Metatron, the Angel, the Prince of the Presence, said to me:

[1]Whenever the Great Beth Din is seated in the *'Araboth Raqia* on high there is no opening of the mouth for anyone in the world save those great princes who are called *H'* by the name of the Holy One, blessed be He.

[2]How many are those princes? Seventy-two princes of the kingdoms of the world besides the Prince of the World who speaks (pleads) in favor of the world before the Holy One, blessed be He, every day, at the hour when the book is opened in which are recorded all the doings of the world, according as it is written (Dan. 7:10): "The judgment was set and the books were opened."

CHAPTER 31

(The attributes of) Justice, Mercy and Truth by the Throne of Judgment

R. Ishmael said: Metatron, the Angel, the Prince of the Presence, said to me:

(1)At the time when the Holy One, blessed be He, is sitting on the Throne, of Judgment, (then) Justice is standing on His right and Mercy on His left and Truth before His face.

(2)And when man enters before Him to judgment, (then) there comes forth from the splendor of the Mercy towards him as (it were) a staff and stands in front of him. Forthwith man falls upon his face, (and) all the angels of destruction fear and tremble before him, according as it is written (Is. 16:5): "And with mercy shall the throne be established, and he shall sit upon it in truth."

CHAPTER 32

The execution of judgment on the wicked. God's sword

R. Ishmael said: Metatron, the Angel, the Prince of the Presence, said to me:

(1)When the Holy One, blessed be He, opens the Book half of which is fire and half flame, (then) they go out from before Him in every moment to execute the judgment on the wicked by His sword (that is) drawn forth out of its sheath and the splendor of which shines like a lightning and pervades the world from one end to the other, as it is written (Is. 15:16): "For by fire will the Lord plead (and by his sword with all flesh)."

(2)And all the inhabitants of the world (*lit.* those who come into the world) fear and tremble before Him, when they behold His sharpened sword like unto a lightning from one end of the world to the other, and sparks and flashes of the size of the stars of *Raqia* going out from it; according as it is written (Deut. 32:41): "If I whet the lightning of my sword".

CHAPTER 33

The angels of Mercy, of Peace and of Destruction by the Throne
of Judgment. The scribes, (vss. 1, 2) The angels by the Throne of
Glory and the fiery rivers under it. (vss. 3-5)

R. Ishmael said: Metatron, the Angel, the Prince of the Presence, said to me:

(1)At the time that the Holy One, blessed be He, is sitting on the Throne of Judgment, (then) the angels of Mercy are standing on His right, the angels of Peace are standing on His left and the angels of Destruction are standing in front of Him.

(2)And one scribe is standing beneath Him, and another scribe above Him.

(3)And the glorious *Seraphim*

A:	E:
surround them like firebrands round about the Throne of Glory.	surround the Throne on its four sides with walls of lightnings, and the *'Ophannim* surround them with firebrands round about the Throne of Glory.

And clouds of fire and clouds of flames compass them to the right and to the left; and the Holy *Chayyoth* carry the Throne of Glory from below: each one with three fingers. The measure of the fingers of each one is 800,000 and 700 times hundred, (and) 66,000 parasangs.

(4)And underneath the feet of the *Chayyoth* seven fiery rivers are running and flowing. And the breadth of each river is 365 thousand parasangs and its depth is 248 thousand myriads of parasangs. Its length is unsearchable and immeasurable.

(5)And each river turns round in a bow in the four directions of 'Araboth *Raqia*, and (from there) it falls down to *Ma'on* and is stayed (?), and from *Ma'on* to *Zebul*, from *Zebul* to *Shechaqim*, from *Shechaqim* to *Raqia'*, from *Raqia'* to *Shamayim* and from *Shamayim* upon the heads of the wicked who are in Gehenna, as it is written (Jer. 23:19): "Behold a whirlwind of the Lord, even his fury, is gone, yea, a whirling tempest; it shall burst upon the head of the wicked"

CHAPTER 34

The different concentric circles round the Chayyoth,
consisting of fire, water, hailstones etc. and of the angels
uttering the Qedushsha responsorium

R. Ishmael said: Metatron; the Angel, the Prince of the Presence, said to me:

(1)The hoofs of the *Chayyoth* are surrounded by seven clouds of burning coals. The clouds of burning coals are surrounded on the outside by seven walls of flame(s). The seven walls of flame(s) are surrounded on the outside by seven walls of hailstones (stones of *'El-gabish*, Ezek. 13:11,13, 28:22). The hailstones are surrounded on the outside by stones of hail (stone of *Barad*). The stones of hail are surrounded on the outside by stones of "the wings of the tempest ". The stones of "the wings of the tempest" are surrounded on the outside by flames of fire. The flames of fire are surrounded by the chambers of the whirlwind. The chambers of the whirlwind are surrounded on the outside by the fire and the water.

[2]Round about the fire and the water are those who utter the "*Holy*". Round about those who utter the "*Holy*" are those who utter the "*Blessed*". Round about those who utter the "*Blessed*" are the bright clouds. The bright clouds are surrounded on the outside by coals of burning jumper; and on the outside surrounding the coals of burning juniper there are thousand camps of fire and ten thousand hosts of flame(s). And between every several camp and every several host there is a cloud, so that they may not be burnt by the fire.

CHAPTER 35

The camps of angels in 'Araboth Raqia: angels, performing the Qedushsha

R. Ishmael said: Metatron, the Angel, the Prince of the Presence, said to me:

[1]506 thousand myriads of camps has the Holy One, blessed be He, in the height of *'Araboth Raqia*. And each camp is (composed of) 496 thousand angels.

[2]And every single angel, the height of his stature is as the great sea; and the appearance of their countenance as the appearance of the lightning, and their eyes as lamps of fire, and their arms and their feet like in color to polished brass and the roaring voice of their words like the voice of a multitude.

[3]And they are all standing before the Throne of Glory in four rows. And the princes of the army are standing at the head of each row.

[4]And some of them utter the "*Holy*" and others utter the "*Blessed*", some of them run as messengers, others are standing in attendance, according as it is written (Dan. 7:10): "Thousand thousands ministered unto him, and ten thousand times ten thousand stood before him: the judgment was set and the books were opened".

[5]And in the hour, when the time draws nigh for to say the "*Holy*", (then) first there goes forth a whirlwind from before the Holy One, blessed be He, and bursts upon the camp of *Shekina* and there arises a great commotion among them, as it is written (Jer. 30:23): "Behold, the whirlwind of the Lord goeth forth with fury, a continuing commotion".

(6)At that moment thousand thousands of them are changed into sparks, thousand thousands of them into firebrands, thousand thousands into flashes, thousand thousands into flames, thousand thousands into males, thousand thousands into females, thousand thousands into winds, thousand thousands into burning fires, thousand thousands into flames, thousand thousands into sparks, thousand thousands into chashmals of light; until they take upon themselves the yoke of the kingdom of heaven, the high and lifted up, of the Creator of them all with fear, dread, awe and trembling, with commotion, anguish, terror and trepidation. Then they are changed again into their former shape to have the fear of their King before them always, as they have set their hearts on saying the Song continually, as it is written (Is. 6:3): "And one cried unto another and said (Holy, Holy, Holy, etc.)".

CHAPTER 36

*The angels bathe in the fiery river before
reciting the 'Song'*

R. Ishmael said: Metatron, the Angel, the Prince of the Presence, said to me:

(1)At the time when the ministering angels desire to say (the) Song, (then) *Nehar di-Nur* (the fiery stream) rises with many "thousand thousands and myriads of myriads" (of angels) of power and strength of fire and it runs and passes under the Throne of Glory, between the camps of the ministering angels and the troops of *'Araboth*.

(2)And all the ministering angels first go down into *Nehar di-Nur*, and they dip themselves in the fire and dip their tongue and their mouth seven times; and after that they go up and put on the garment of '*Machaqe Samal*' and cover themselves with cloaks of *chashmal* and stand in four rows over against the Throne of Glory, in all the heavens.

CHAPTER 38

The four camps of Shekina and their surroundings

R. Ishmael said: Metatron, the Angel, the Prince of the Presence, said to me:

(1)In the seven Halls there are standing four chariots of *Shekina*, and before each one are standing the four camps of *Shekina*. Between each camp a river of fire is continually flowing.

(2)Between each river there are bright clouds [surrounding them], and between each cloud there are put up pillars of brimstone. Between one pillar and another there are standing flaming wheels, surrounding them. And between one wheel and another there are flames of fire round about. Between one flame and another there are treasuries of lightnings; behind the treasuries of lightnings are the wings of the storm-wind. Behind the wings of the storm-wind are the chambers of the tempest; behind the chambers of the tempest there are winds, voices, thunders, sparks [upon] sparks and earthquakes [upon] earthquakes.

CHAPTER 38

*The fear that befalls all the heavens at the sound of the 'Holy,'
esp. the heavenly bodies. These appeased by the Prince of the
World*

R. Ishmael said: Metatron, the Angel, the Prince of the Presence, said to me:

(1)At the time, when the ministering angels utter (the Thrice) Holy, then all the pillars of the heavens and their sockets do tremble, and the gates of the Halls of 'Araboth *Raqia* are shaken and the foundations of *Shechaqim* and the Universe (*Tebel*) are moved, and the orders of *Ma'on* and the chambers of *Makon* quiver, and all the orders of *Raqia* and the constellations and the planets are dismayed, and the globes of the sun and the moon haste away and flee out of their courses and run 12,000 parasangs and seek to throw themselves down from heaven, (2)by reason of the roaring voice of their chant, and the noise of their praise and the sparks and lightnings that go forth from their faces; as it is written (Ps. 26:18): "The voice of thy thunder was in the heaven (the lightnings lightened the world, the earth trembled and shook)".

(3)Until the prince of the world calls them, saying: "Be ye quiet in your place! Fear not because of the ministering angels who sing the Song before the Holy One, blessed be He". As it is written (Job 38:7): "When the morning stars sang together and all the children of heaven shouted for joy".

CHAPTER 39

*The explicit names fly off from the Throne and all the various
angelic hosts prostrate themselves before it at the time of the
Qedushsha*

R. Ishmael said: Metatron, the Angel, the Prince of the Presence, said to me:

(1)When the ministering angels utter the "*Holy*" then all the explicit names that are graven with a flaming style on the Throne of Glory fly off like eagles, with sixteen wings. And they surround and compass the Holy One, blessed be He, on the four sides of the place of His *Shekina*.

(2)And the angels of the host, and the flaming Servants, and the mighty '*Ophannim*, and the *Kerubim* of the *Shekina*, and the Holy *Chayyoth*, and the *Seraphim*, and the '*Er'ellim*, and the *Taphsarim* and the troops of consuming fire, and the fiery armies, and the flaming hosts, and the holy princes, adorned with crowns, clad in kingly majesty, wrapped in glory, girt with loftiness, fall upon their faces three times, saying: "Blessed be the name of His glorious kingdom forever and ever".

CHAPTER 40

*The ministering angels rewarded with crowns, when uttering
the "Holy" in its right order, and punished by consuming fire
if not. New ones created in the stead of the consumed angels*

R. Ishmael said: Metatron, the Angel, the Prince of the Presence, said to me:

(1)When the ministering angels say "*Holy*" before the Holy One, blessed be He, in the proper way, then the servants of His Throne, the attendants of His Glory, go forth with great mirth from under the Throne of Glory. (2)And they all carry in their hands, each one of them thousand thousand and ten thousand times ten thousand crowns of stars, similar in appearance to the planet Venus, and put them on the ministering angels and the great princes who utter the "*Holy*". Three crowns they put on each one of them: one crown because they say "*Holy*", another crown, because they say "*Holy, Holy*", and a third crown because they say "*Holy, Holy, Holy, is the Lord of Hosts*".

(3)And in the moment that they do not utter the "*Holy*" in the right order, a consuming fire goes forth from the little finger of the Holy One, blessed be He, and falls down in the midst of their ranks and is divided into 496 thousand parts corresponding to the four camps of the ministering angels, and consumes them in one moment, as it is written (Ps. 97:3): "A fire goeth before him and burneth up his adversaries round about".

[4]After that the Holy One, blessed be He, opens His mouth and speaks one word and creates others in their stead, new ones like them. And each one stands before His Throne of Glory, uttering the "*Holy*", as it is written (Lam. 3:23): "They are new every morning; great is thy faithfulness".

CHAPTER 41

Metatron shows R. Ishmael the letters engraved on the
Throne of Glory by which letters everything in heaven and
earth has been created

R. Ishmael said: Metatron, the Angel, the Prince of the Presence, said to me:

[1]Come and behold the letters by which the heaven and the earth were created,

> the letters by which were created the mountains and hills,
> the letters by which were created the seas and rivers,
> the letters by which were created the trees and herbs,
> the letters by which were created the planets and the constellations,
> the letters by which were created the globe of the moon and the globe of the sun, Orion, the Pleiades and all the different luminaries of *Raqia*.

[2]the letters by which were created the Throne of Glory and the Wheels of the *Merkaba*, the letters by which were created the necessities of the worlds,

[3]the letters by which were created wisdom, understanding, knowledge, prudence, meekness and righteousness by which the whole world is sustained.

[4]And I walked by his side and he took me by his hand and raised me upon his wings and showed me those letters, all of them, that are graven with a flaming style on the Throne of Glory: and sparks go forth from them and cover all the chambers of *'Araboth*.

CHAPTER 42

Instances of polar opposites kept in balance by several Divine
Names and other similar wonders

R. Ishmael said: Metatron, the Angel, the Prince of the Presence, said to me:

(1)Come and I will show thee, where the waters are suspended in the highest, where fire is burning in the midst of hail, where lightnings lighten out of the midst of snowy mountains, where thunders are roaring in the celestial heights, where a flame is burning in the midst of the burning fire and where voices make themselves heard in the midst of thunder and earthquake.

(2)Then I went by his side and he took me by his hand and lifted me up on his wings and showed me all those things. I beheld the waters suspended on high in *'Araboth Raqia* by (force of) the name *YAH 'EHYE 'ASHER 'EHYE* (Jah, I am that I am), and their fruits going down from heaven and watering the face of the world, as it is written (Ps. 104:13): "(He watereth the mountains from his chambers:) the earth is satisfied with the fruit of thy work".

(3)And I saw fire and snow and hailstone that were mingled together within each other and yet were undamaged, by (force of) the name *'ESH 'OKELA* (consuming fire), as it is written (Deut. 4:24): "For the Lord, thy God, is a consuming fire".

(4)And I saw lightnings that were lightening out of mountains of snow and yet were not damaged (quenched), by (force of) the name *YAH SUR 'OLAMIM* (Jah, the everlasting rock), as it is written (Is. 26:4): "For in Jah, *YHWH*, the everlasting rock".

(5)And I saw thunders and voices that were roaring in the midst of fiery flames and were not damaged (silenced), by (force of) the name *'EL-SHADDAI RABBA* (the Great God Almighty) as it is written (Gen. 17:1): "I am God Almighty".

(6)And I beheld a flame (and) a glow (glowing flames) that were flaming and glowing in the midst of burning fire, and yet were not damaged (devoured), by (force of) the name *YAD 'AL KES YAH* (the hand upon the Throne of the Lord) as it is written (Ex. 17:16): "And he said: for the hand is upon the Throne of the Lord ".

(7)And I beheld rivers of fire in the midst of rivers of water and they were not damaged (quenched) by (force of) the name *'OSE SHALOM* (Maker of Peace) as it is written (Job 25:2): "He maketh peace in his high places". For he makes peace between the fire and the water, between the hail and the fire, between the wind and the cloud, between the earthquake and the sparks.

CHAPTER 43

Metatron shows R. Ishmael the abode of the unborn spirits
and of the spirits of the righteous dead

R. Ishmael said: Metatron said to me:

[1]Come and I will show thee where are the spirits of the righteous that have been created and have returned, and the spirits of the righteous that have not yet been created.

[2]And he lifted me up to his side, took me by his hand and lifted me up near the Throne of Glory by the place of the *Shekina*; and he revealed the Throne of Glory to me, and he showed me the spirits that have been created and had returned: and they were flying above the Throne of Glory before the Holy One, blessed be He.

[3]After that I went to interpret the following verse of Scripture and I found in what is written (Isa. 57:16): "for the spirit clothed itself before me, and the souls I have made" that ("for the spirit was clothed before me") means the spirits that have been created in the chamber of creation of the righteous and that have returned before the Holy One, blessed be He; (and the words:) "and the souls I have made" refer to the spirits of the righteous that have not yet been created in the chamber (*GUPH*).

CHAPTER 44

Metatron shows R. Ishmael the abode of the wicked and the
intermediate in Sheol. (vss. 1-6) The Patriarchs pray for the
deliverance of Israel (vss. 7-10)

R. Ishmael said: Metatron, the Angel, the Prince of the Presence, said to me:

[1]Come and I will show thee the spirits of the wicked and the spirits of the intermediate where they are standing, and the spirits of the intermediate, whither they go down, and the spirits of the wicked, where they go down.

[2]And he said to me: The spirits of the wicked go down to She'ol by the hands of two angels of destruction: ZA'APHIEL and SIMKIEL are their names. [3]SIMKIEL is appointed over the intermediate to support them and purify them because of the great mercy of the Prince of the Place (*Maqom*). ZA'APHIEL is appointed over the spirits of the wicked in order to cast them down from the presence of the Holy One, blessed be

He, and from the splendor of the *Shekina* to She'ol, to be punished in the fire of Gehenna with staves of burning coal.

(4)And I went by his side, and he took me by his hand and showed me all of them with his fingers.

(5)And I beheld the appearance of their faces (and, lo, it was) as the appearance of children of men, and their bodies like eagles. And not only that but (furthermore) the color of the countenance of the intermediate was like pale gray on account of their deeds, for there are stains upon them until they have become cleaned from their iniquity in the fire.

(6)And the color of the wicked was like the bottom of a pot on account of the wickedness of their doings.

(7)And I saw the spirits of the Patriarchs Abraham Isaac and Jacob and the rest of the righteous whom they have brought up out of their graves and who have ascended to the Heaven (*Raqia*). And they were praying before the Holy One, blessed be He, saying in their prayer: "Lord of the Universe! How long wilt thou sit upon (thy) Throne like a mourner in the days of his mourning with thy right hand behind thee and not deliver thy children and reveal thy Kingdom in the world? And for how long wilt thou have no pity upon thy children who are made slaves among the nations of the world? Nor upon thy right hand that is behind thee wherewith thou didst stretch out the heavens and the earth and the heavens of heavens? When wilt thou have compassion?"

(8)Then the Holy One, blessed be He, answered everyone of them, saying: "Since these wicked do sin so and so, and transgress with such and such transgressions against me, how could I deliver my great Right Hand in the downfall by their hands (caused by them).

(9)In that moment Metatron called me and spake to me: "My servant! Take the books, and read their evil doings!" Forthwith I took the books and read their doings and there were to be found 36 transgressions (written down) with regard to each wicked one and besides, that they have transgressed all the letters in the Tora, as it is written (Dan. 9:11): "Yea, all Israel have transgressed thy Law". It is not written 'al torateka but 'et (את) torateka, for they have transgressed from 'Aleph (א) to Taw (ת), 40 statutes have they transgressed for each letter.

(10)Forthwith Abraham, Isaac and Jacob wept. Then said to them the Holy One, blessed be He: "Abraham, my beloved, Isaac, my Elect one, Jacob, my firstborn! How can I now deliver them from among the nations of the world?" And forthwith MIKAEL, the Prince of Israel, cried and wept with a loud voice and said (Ps. 10:1): "Why standest thou afar off, O Lord?"

CHAPTER 45

Metatron shows R. Ishmael past and future events recorded
on the Curtain of the Throne

R. Ishmael said: Metatron said to me:

(1)Come, and I will show thee the Curtain of *MAQOM* (the Divine Majesty) which is spread before the Holy One, blessed be He, (and) whereon are graven all the generations of the world and all their doings, both what they have done and what they will do until the end of all generations.

(2)And I went, and he showed it to me pointing it out with his fingers like a father who teaches his children the letters of Tora. And I saw each generation,

> the rulers of each generation,
> and the heads of each generation,
> the shepherds of each generation,
> the oppressors (drivers) of each generation,
> the keepers of each generation,
> the scourgers of each generation,
> the overseers of each generation,
> the judges of each generation,
> the court officers of each generation,
> the teachers of each generation,
> the supporters of each generation,
> the chiefs of each generation,
> the presidents of academies of each generation,
> the magistrates of each generation,
> the princes of each generation,
> the counselors of each generation,
> the nobles of each generation,
> and the men of might of each generation,
> the elders of each generation,
> and the guides of each generation.

(3)And I saw Adam, his generation, their doings and their thoughts,
Noah and his generation, their doings and their thoughts,
and the generation of the flood, their doings and their thoughts,
Shem and his generation, their doings and their thoughts,
Nimrod and the generation of the confusion of tongues, and his generation, their doings and their thoughts,

Abraham and his generation, their doings and their thoughts,
Isaac and his generation, their doings and their thoughts,
Ishmael and his generation, their doings and their thoughts,
Jacob and his generation, their doings and their thoughts,
Joseph and his generation, their doings and their thoughts,
the tribes and their generation, their doings and their thoughts,
Amram and his generation, their doings and their thoughts,
Moses and his generation, their doings and their thoughts,

(4) Aaron and Mirjam their works and their doings,
the princes and the elders, their works and doings,
Joshua and his generation, their works and doings,
the judges and their generation, their works and doings,
Eli and his generation, their works and doings,
"Phinehas, their (?) works and doings,
Elkanah and his generation, their works and their doings,
Samuel and his generation, their works and doings,
the kings of Judah with their generations, their works and their doings,
the kings of Israel and their generations, their works and their doings,
the princes of Israel, their works and their doings; the princes of the nations of the world, their works and their doings,
the heads of the councils of Israel, their works and their doings;
the heads of (the councils in) the nations of the world, their generations, their works and their doings;
the rulers of Israel and their generation, their works and their doings;
the nobles of Israel and their generation, their works and their doings; the nobles of the nations of the world and their generation(s), their works and their doings;
the men of reputation in Israel, their generation, their works and their doings;
the judges of Israel, their generation, their works and their doings;
the judges of the nations of the world and their generation, their works and their doings;
the teachers of children in Israel, their generations, their works and their doings; the teachers of children in the nations of the world, their generations, their works and their doings;
the counselors (interpreters) of Israel, their generation, their works and their doings;
the counselors (interpreters) of the nations of the world, their generation, their works and their doings; all the prophets of Israel, their generation, their works and their doings;
all the prophets of the nations of the world, their generation, their works and their doings;

(5)and all the fights and wars that the nations of the world wrought against the people of Israel in the time of their kingdom.

And I saw Messiah, son of Joseph, and his generation "and their" works and their doings that they will do against the nations of the world. And I saw Messiah, son of David, and his generation, and all the fights and wars, and their works and their doings that they will do with Israel both for good and evil. And I saw all the fights and wars that Gog and Magog will fight in the days of Messiah, and all that the Holy One, blessed be He, will do with them in the time to come.

(6)And all the rest of all the leaders of the generations and all the works of the generations both in Israel and in the nations of the world, both what is done and what will be done hereafter to all generations until the end of time, (all) were graven on the Curtain of *MAQOM*. And I saw all these things with my eyes; and after I had seen it, I opened my mouth in praise of *MAQOM* (the Divine Majesty) (saying thus, Eccl. 8:4, 5): "For the King's word hath power (and who may say unto him: What doest thou?) Whoso keepeth the commandments shall know no evil thing". And I said: (Ps. 104:24) "O Lord, how manifold are thy works!"

CHAPTER 46

The place of the stars shown to R. Ishmael

R. Ishmael said: Metatron said to me:

(1)(Come and I will show thee) the space of the stars that are standing in *Raqia* night by night in fear of the Almighty (*MAQOM*) and (I will show thee) where they go and where the stand.

(2)I walked by his side, and he took me by his hand and pointed out all to me with his fingers. And they were standing on sparks of flames round the *Merkaba* of the Almighty (*MAQOM*). What did Metatron do? At that moment he clapped his hands and chased them off from their place. Forthwith they flew off on flaming wings, rose and fled from the four sides of the Throne of the *Merkaba*, and (as they flew) he told me the names of every single one. As it is written (Ps. 147:4): "He telleth the number of the stars; he giveth them all their names", teaching, that the Holy One, blessed be He, has given a name to each one of them.

(3)And they all enter in counted order under the guidance of (lit. through, by the hands of) RAHATIEL to *Raqia ha-shSHamayim* to serve the world. And they go out in counted order to praise the Holy One, blessed be He, with songs and hymns, according as it is written (Ps. 19:1): "The heavens declare the glory of God".

(4)But in the time to come the Holy One, blessed be He, will create them anew, as it is written (Lam. 3:23): "They are new every morning". And they open their mouth and utter a song. Which is the song that they utter? (Ps. 8:3): "When I consider thy heavens".

CHAPTER 47

Metatron shows R. Ishmael the spirits of the punished angels

R. Ishmael said: Metatron said to me:

(1)Come and I will show thee the souls of the angels and the spirits of the ministering servants whose bodies have been burnt in the fire of *MAQOM* (the Almighty) that goes forth from his little finger. And they have been made into fiery coals in the midst of the fiery river (*Nehar di-Nur*). But their spirits and their souls are standing behind the *Shekina*.

(2)Whenever the ministering angels utter a song at a wrong time or as not appointed to be sung they are burnt and consumed by the fire of their Creator and by a flame from their Maker,

A:	*E:*
in the places (chambers) of the whirlwind, for it blows upon them and drives them	in their place (= on the spot); and a whirlwind blows upon them and throws them down

into the *Nehar di-Nur*; and there they are made into numerous mountains of burning coal. But their spirit and their soul return to their Creator, and all are standing behind their Master.

(3)And I went by his side and he took me by his hand; and he showed me all the souls of the angels and the spirits of the ministering servants who were standing behind the *Shekina* upon wings of the whirlwind and walls of fire surrounding them.

(4)At that moment Metatron opened to me the gates of the walls within which they were standing behind the *Shekina*, And I lifted up my eyes and saw them, and behold, the likeness of every one was as (that of) angels and their wings like birds' (wings), made out of flames, the work of burning fire. In that moment I opened my mouth in praise of *MAQOM* and said (Ps. 92:5): "How great are thy works, O Lord".

CHAPTER 48^(A)

*Metatron shows R. Ishmael the Right Hand of the Most High,
now inactive behind Him, but in the future destined to work
the deliverance of Israel*

R. Ishmael said: Metatron said to me:

⁽¹⁾Come, and I will show thee the Right Hand of *MAQOM*, laid behind (Him) because of the destruction of the Holy Temple; from which all kinds of splendor and light shine forth and by which the 955 heavens were created; and whom not even the *Seraphim* and the 'Ophannim' are permitted (to behold), until the day of salvation shall arrive.

⁽²⁾And I went by his side and he took me by his hand and showed me (the Right Hand of *MAQOM*), with all manner of praise, rejoicing and song: and no mouth can tell its praise, and no eye can behold it, because of its greatness, dignity, majesty, glory and beauty.

⁽³⁾And not only that, but all the souls of the righteous who are counted worthy to behold the joy of Jerusalem, they are standing by it, praising and praying before it three times every day, saying (Is. 51:9): "Awake, awake, put on strength, O arm of the Lord" according as it is written (Is. 63:12): "He caused his glorious arm to go at the right hand of Moses".

⁽⁴⁾In that moment the Right Hand of *MAQOM* was weeping. And there went forth from its five fingers five rivers of tears and fell down into the great sea and shook the whole world, according as it is written (Is. 24:19, 20): "The earth is utterly broken (1), the earth is clean dissolved (2), the earth is moved exceedingly (3), the earth shall stagger like a drunken man (4) and shall be moved to and fro like a hut (5)", five times corresponding to the fingers of his Great Right Hand.

⁽⁵⁾But when the Holy One, blessed be He, sees, that there is no righteous man in the generation, and no pious man (*Chasid*) on earth, and no justice in the hands of men; and (that there is) no man like unto Moses, and no intercessor as Samuel who could pray before *MAQOM* for the salvation and for the deliverance, and for His Kingdom, that it be revealed in the whole world; and for His great Right Hand that He put it before Himself again to work great salvation by it for Israel,

⁽⁶⁾then forthwith will the Holy One, blessed be He, remember His own justice, favor, mercy and grace: and He will deliver His great Arm by himself, and His righteousness will support Him. According as it is written (Is. 59:16): "And he saw, that there was no man"—(that is:) like unto Moses who prayed countless times for Israel in the desert and averted the (Divine) decrees from them—"and he wondered, that there was no intercessor"—like unto Samuel who entreated the Holy One, blessed be He, and called unto Him and he answered him and fulfilled his desire, even if it was not fit (in accordance with the Divine plan), according as it is written (1 Sam. 12:17): "Is it not wheat-harvest today? I will call unto the Lord".

⁽⁷⁾And not only that, but He joined fellowship with Moses in every place, as it is written (Ps. 99:6): "Moses and Aaron among His priests". And again it is written (Jer. 15:1): "Though Moses and Samuel stood before me" (Is. 63:5): "Mine own arm brought salvation unto me".

⁽⁸⁾Said the Holy One, blessed be He in that hour: "How long shall I wait for the children of men to work salvation according to their righteousness for my arm? For my own sake and for the sake of my merit and righteousness will I deliver my arm and by it redeem my children from among the nations of the world. As it is written (Is. 48:11): "For my own sake will I do it. For how should my name be profaned".

⁽⁹⁾In that moment will the Holy One, blessed be He, reveal His Great Arm and show it to the nations of the world: for its length is as the length of the world and its breadth is as the width of the world. And the appearance of its splendor is like unto the splendor of the sunshine in its might, in the summer solstice.

⁽¹⁰⁾Forthwith Israel will be saved from among the nations of the world. And Messiah will appear unto them and He will bring them up to Jerusalem with great joy. And not only that but

A:

they will eat and drink for they will glorify the Kingdom of Messiah, of the house of David, in the four quarters of the world. And the nations of the world will not prevail against them,

E:.

Israel will come from the four quarters of the world and eat with Messiah. But the nations of the world shall not eat with them,

as it is written (Is. 52:10): "The Lord hath made bare his holy arm in the eyes of all the nations; and all the ends of the earth shall see the salvation of our God". And again (Deut. 32:12): "The Lord alone did lead him, and there was no strange god with him". (Zech. 14:9): "And the Lord shall be king over all the earth".

CHAPTER 48 (cont.) (B)

*The Divine Names that go forth from the Throne of Glory,
crowned and escorted by numerous angelic hosts through the
heavens and back again to the Throne—the angels sing the
'Holy' and the 'Blessed'*

AEFGH:

(1)These are the names of the Holy One, blessed be He,

K:

These are the seventy-two names written on the heart of the Holy One, blessed be He: SS, SeDeQ {righteousness}, SaHI'eL SUR {Is. 26:4}, SBI, SaDdIQ {righteous}, S'Ph, SHN, SeBa'oTh {Lord of Hosts}, ShaDdaY {God Almighty}, 'eLoHIM {God}, YHWH, SH, DGUL, W'DOM, SSS", 'YW, 'Y', 'HW, HB, YaH, HW, WWW, SSS, PPP, NN, HH, HaY {living}, HaY, ROKeB 'aRaBOTh {riding upon the Araboth, Ps. 68:5}, YH, HH, WH, MMM, NNN, HWW, YH, YHH, HPhS, H'S, 'I, W, S", Z', ''', QQQ {Holy, Holy, Holy}, QShR, BW, ZK, GINUR, GINURYa', Y' YOD, 'aLePh, H'N, P'P, R'W, YYW, YYW, BBS, DDD, TTT, KKK, KLL, SYS, 'TT, BShKMLW {= blessed be the Name of His glorious kingdom forever and ever}, completed for MeLeK Ha'OLaM {the King of the Universe}, BRH LB' {the beginning of Wisdom for the children of men}, BNLK W' 'Y {blessed be He who gives strength to the weary and increaseth strength to them that have no might, Is. 40:29}

that go forth (adorned) with numerous crowns of fire with numerous crowns of flame, with numerous crowns of chashmal, with numerous crowns of lightning from before the Throne of Glory. And with them (there are) thousand hundreds of power (i.e. powerful angels) who escort them like a king

AE:

with honor and pillars of fire and cloud(s), and pillars of flame, and with lightnings of radiance and with the likeness of (the)

FG:

with trembling and dread, with awe and shivering, with honor and majesty and fear, with terror, with greatness and dignity, with glory and strength, with understanding and knowledge and with a pillar of fire and a pillar of flame and lightning and their light is as lightnings of light *chashmal.*   *and with the likeness of the chashmal.*

(2)And they give glory unto them and they answer and cry before them: Holy, Holy, Holy. And they roll (convoy) them through every heaven as mighty and honored princes. And when they bring them all back to the place of the Throne of Glory, then all the Chayyoth by the Merkaba open their mouth in praise of His glorious name, saying: "Blessed be the name of His glorious kingdom forever and ever".

CHAPTER 48 (cont.) (c)

An Enoch-Metatron piece

AEFGH:

(1)Aleph I made him strong, I took him, I appointed him: (namely) Metatron, my servant who is one (unique) among all the children of heaven. I made him strong in the generation of the first Adam. But when I beheld the men of the generation of the flood, that they were corrupt, then I went and removed my Shekina from among them. And I lifted it up on high with the sound of a trumpet and with a shout, as it is written (Ps. 47:6): "God is gone up with a shout, the Lord with the sound of a trumpet".

(2)"And I took him": (that is) Enoch, the

son of Jared, from among them. And I lifted him up with the sound of a trumpet and with a teru'a (shout) to the high heavens, to be my witness together with the *Chayyoth* by the *Merkaba* in the world

K:

(1)"I seized him, and I took him and I appointed him"—that is Enoch, the son of Jared, whose name is Metatron *(2)*and I took him from among the children of men *(5)*and made him a Throne over against my Throne. Which is the size of that Throne? Seventy thousand parasangs (all) of fire. *(9)*I committed unto him 70 angels corresponding to the nations (of the world) and I gave into his charge all the household above and below. *(7)*And I committed to him Wisdom and Intelligence more than (to) all the angels. And I called his name "the LESSER

YAH", whose name is by Gematria 71. And I arranged for him all the works of Creation. And I made his power to transcend (lit. I made for him power more than) all the ministering angels. (Ends K.)

to come.

Lm (begins here):

(3)I appointed him over all the treasuries and stores: that I have in every heaven. And I committed into his hand the keys of every several one.

(3)He committed unto Metatron—that is Enoch, the son of Jared—all treasuries. And I appointed him over all the stores that I have in every heaven. And I committed into his hands I the keys of each heavenly store.

(4)I made (of) him the prince over all the princes and a minister of the Throne of Glory (and) the Halls of 'Araboth: to open their doors to me, and (of) the Throne of Glory, to exalt and arrange it; (and I appointed him over) the Holy *Chayyoth* to wreathe crowns upon their heads; the majestic *'Ophannim*, to crown them with strength and glory; the honored *Kerubim*, to clothe: them in majesty; over the radiant sparks, to make them to shine with splendor and brilliance; over the flaming *Seraphim*, to cover them with highness; the *Chashmallim* of light, to make them radiant with light and to prepare the seat for me every morning

(4)I made (of) him the prince over all the princes, and I made (of) him a minister of my Throne of Glory, to provide for and arrange the Holy *Chayyoth*, to wreathe crowns for them (to crown them with crowns), to clothe them with honor and majesty to prepare for them a seat

A:

as I sit upon the Throne of Glory. And to extol and magnify my glory in the height of my power; (and I have committed unto him) the secrets of above and the secrets of below (heavenly secrets and earthly secrets).

FGH:

when I am seated upon my Throne in glory and, dignity that he may see my glory in the height of my power, in the secrets of above and in the secrets of below.

Lm:

when he is sitting on his throne to magnify his glory in the height.

AFGH:

[5] I made him higher than all. The height of his stature, in the midst of all (who are) high of stature (I made) seventy thousand parasangs. I made his Throne great by the majesty of my Throne. And I increased its glory by the honor of my glory.

[6] I transformed his flesh into torches of fire, and all the bones of his body into fiery coals; and I made the appearance of his eyes as the lightning, and the light of his eyebrows as the imperishable light. I made his face bright as the splendor of the sun, and his eyes as the splendor of the Throne of Glory.

[7] I made honor and majesty his clothing, beauty and highness his covering cloak and a royal crown of 500 by (times) 500 parasangs (his) diadem.

Lm:

[5] The height of his stature among all those (that are) of high stature (is) seventy thousand parasangs. And I made his glory great as the majesty of my glory

[6] and the brilliance of his eyes as the splendor of the Throne of Glory

[7] his garment honor and majesty, his royal crown 500 by 500 parasangs.

AFGHLm:

And I put upon him of my honor, my majesty and the splendor of my glory that is upon my Throne of Glory. I called him the LESSER YHWH, the Prince of the Presence, the Knower of Secrets: for every secret did I reveal to him as a father and all mysteries declared I unto him in uprightness.

(8)I set up his throne at the door of my Hall that he may sit and judge the heavenly household on high. And I placed every prince before him, to receive authority from him, to perform his will.

(9)Seventy names did I take from (my) names and called him by them to enhance his glory.

Seventy princes gave I into his hand, to command unto them my precepts and my words in every language:

AFGH:

to abase by his word the proud to the ground, and to exalt by the utterance of his lips the humble to the height; to smite kings by his speech, to turn kings away from their paths, to set up (the) rulers over their dominion as it is written (Dan. 2:21): "and he changeth the times and the seasons," and to give wisdom unto all the wise of the world and understanding (and) knowledge to all who understand knowledge, as it is written (Dan. 2:21): "and knowledge to them that know understanding", to reveal to them the secrets of my words and to teach the decree of my righteous judgment, (10)as it is written (Is. 55:11):

Lm:

and to abase the proud to the ground

and to exalt the humble to the height

and to smite kings

and to bring rulers low

and to set up kings and rulers

and he changeth the times and the seasons

he removeth kings and setteth up kings

he giveth wisdom unto the wise

and knowledge to them that know understanding

and I appointed him to reveal secrets and to teach judgment and justice,

AFGHLm:

"so shall my word be that goeth forth out of my mouth; it shall not return unto me void but shall accomplish (that which I please)". "E'eseh' (I shall accomplish) is not written here, but "asah' (he shall accomplish), meaning, that whatever word and whatever utterance goes forth from before the Holy One, blessed be He, Metatron stands and carries it out. And he establishes the decrees of the Holy One, blessed be He. (Here the Lm version of fragment c ends.)

[(11)"And he shall make to prosper that which I sent ". 'Asliᵃh (will make to prosper) is not written here, but wᵉhisliᵃh (and he shall make to prosper), teaching, that whatever decree goes forth from before the Holy One, blessed be He, concerning a man, as soon as he make repentance, they do not execute it (upon him) but upon another, wicked man, as it is written (Prov. 11:8): "*The righteous is delivered out of trouble, and the wicked cometh in his stead*".]

(12)And not only that but Metatron sits three hours every day in the high heavens, and he gathers all the souls of those dead who died in their mother's womb, and the sucklings who died on their mother's breasts, and of the scholars who died over the five books of the Law. And he brings them under the Throne of Glory and places them in companies, divisions and classes round the Presence: and he teaches them the Law, and (the books) of Wisdom, and Haggada and Tradition and finishes (completes) their instruction (education) [for them]. As it is written (Is. 28:9): "Whom will he teach knowledge? and whom will he make to understand tradition? them that are weaned from the milk and drawn from the breasts".

CHAPTER 48[(D)]

The names of Metatron. The treasuries of Wisdom opened to Moses on mount Sinai. The angels protest against Metatron for revealing the secrets to Moses and are answered and rebuked by God. The chain of tradition and the power of the transmitted mysteries to heal diseases

[(1)]Seventy names has Metatron which the Holy One, blessed be He, took from his own name and put upon him. And these they are:

$_1$YeHOEL YaH, $_2$YeHOEL, $_3$YOPHIEL and $_4$Yophphiel, and $_5$'APHPHIEL and $_6$MaRGeZIEL, $_7$GIPpUYEL, $_8$Pa'aZIEL, $_9$'A'aH, $_{100}$PeRIEL, $_{11}$TaTRIEL, $_{12}$TaBKIEL, $_{13}$'W, $_{14}$YHWH, $_{15}$DH, $_{16}$WHYH, $_{17}$eBeD, $_{18}$DiBbURIEL, $_{19}$aPh'aPIEL, $_{20}$SPPIEL, $_{21}$PaSPaSIEL, $_{22}$SeNeGRON, $_{23}$MeTaTRON, $_{24}$SOGDIN, $_{25}$'ADRIGON, $_{26}$'ASUM, $_{27}$SaQPaM, $_{28}$SaQTaM, $_{29}$MIGON, $_{30}$MITTON, $_{31}$MOTTRON, $_{32}$ROSPHIM, $_{33}$QINOTh, $_{34}$ChaTaTYaH $_{35}$DeGaZYaH, $_{36}$PSPYaH, $_{37}$'BSKNYH, $_{38}$MZRG.., $_{39}$BaRaD.., $_{40}$MKRKK, $_{41}$MSPRD, $_{42}$ChShG, $_{43}$ChShB, $_{44}$MNRTTT, $_{45}$BSYRYM, $_{46}$MITMON, $_{47}$TITMON, $_{48}$PiSQON, $_{49}$SaPhSaPhYaH', $_{50}$ZRCh, $_{51}$ZRChYaH, $_{52}$'B', $_{53}$BeYaH, $_{54}$HBH BeYaH, $_{55}$PeLeT, $_{56}$PLTYaH, $_{57}$RaBRaBYaH, $_{58}$ChaS, $_{59}$ChaSYaH, $_{60}$TaPhTaPhYaH, $_{61}$TaMTaMYaH, $_{62}$SeHaSYaH, $_{63}$'IR'URYaH, $_{64}$aL'aLYaH, $_{65}$BaZRIDYaH, $_{66}$SaTSaTKYaH, $_{67}$SaSDYaH, $_{68}$RaZRaZYaH, $_{69}$BaZRaZYaH, $_{70}$'aRIMYaH, $_{71}$SBHYaH, $_{72}$SBIBKHYH, $_{73}$SiMKaM, $_{74}$YaHSeYaH, $_{75}$SSBIBYaH, $_{76}$SaBKaSBeYaH, $_{77}$QeLILQaLYaH, $_{78}$KIHHH, $_{79}$HHYH, $_{80}$WH, $_{81}$WHYH, $_{82}$ZaKklKYaH, $_{83}$TUTRISYaH, $_{84}$SURYaH, $_{85}$ZeH, $_{86}$PeNIRHYaH, $_{87}$Z'ZI'H, $_{88}$GaL RaZaYYa, $_{89}$MaMLIKYaH, $_{90}$'TTYaH, $_{91}$eMeQ, $_{92}$QaMYaH, $_{93}$MeKaPpeRYaH, $_{94}$PeRISHYaH, $_{95}$SePhaM, $_{96}$GBIR, $_{97}$GiBbORYaH, $_{98}$GOR, $_{99}$GORYaH, $_{100}$ZIW,

101'OKBaR, the 102LESSER YHWH, after the name of his Master, (Ex. 23:21) "for my name is in him", 103RaBIBIEL, 104TUMIEL, 105Segansakkiel, the Prince of Wisdom.

(2)*And why is he called by the name Sagnesakiel? Because all the treasuries of wisdom are committed in his hand.*

(3)*And all of them were opened to Moses on Sinai, so that he learnt them during the forty days, while he was standing (remaining}: the Torah in the seventy aspects of the seventy tongues, the Prophets in the seventy aspects of the seventy tongues, the Writings in the seventy aspects of the seventy tongues, "the Halakas in the seventy aspects of the seventy tongues, the Traditions in the seventy aspects of the seventy tongues, the Haggadas in the seventy aspects of the seventy tongues and the Toseftas in the seventy aspects of the seventy tongues.*

(4)*But as soon as the forty days were ended, he forgot all of them in one moment. Then the Holy One, blessed be He, called Yephiphyah, the Prince of the Law, and (through him) they were given to Moses as a gift. As it is written (Deut. 10:4): "and the Lord gave them unto me". And after that it remained with him. And whence do we know, that it remained (in his memory)? Because it is written (Mal. 4:4): "Remember ye the Law of Moses my servant which I commanded unto him in Horeb for all Israel, even my statutes and judgments". 'The Law of Moses': that is the Tora, the Prophets and the Writings, 'statutes': that is the Halakas and Traditions, 'judgments'; that is the Haggadas and the Toseftas. And all of them were given to Moses on high on Sinai.*

(5)*These seventy names (are) a reflection of the Explicit Name(s) on the Merkaba which are graven upon the Throne of Glory. For the Holy One, blessed be He, took from His Explicit Name(s) and put upon the name of Metatron: Seventy Names of His by which the ministering angels call the King of the kings of kings, blessed be He, in the high heavens, and twenty-two letters that are on the ring upon his finger with which are sealed the destinies of the princes of kingdoms on high in greatness and power and with which are sealed the lots of the Angel of Death, and the destinies of every nation and tongue.*

(6)*Said Metatron, the Angel, the Prince of the Presence; the Angel, the Prince of the Wisdom; the Angel, the Prince of the Understanding; the Angel, the Prince of the Kings; the Angel, the Prince of the Rulers; the angel, the Prince of the Glory; the angel, the Prince of the high ones, and of the princes, the exalted, great and honored ones, in heaven and on earth:*

(7)*"H, the God of Israel, is my witness in this thing, (that) when I revealed this secret to Moses, then all the hosts in every heaven on high raged against me and said to me:* (8)*Why dost thou reveal this secret to a son of man, born of woman, tainted and unclean, a man of a putrefying drop, the secret by which were created heaven and earth, the sea and the dry land, the mountains and hills, the rivers and springs, Gehenna of fire and hail, the Garden of Eden and the Tree of Life; and by which were formed Adam and Eve, and the cattle, and the wild beasts, and the fowl of the air, and the fish of the sea, and Behemoth and*

Leviathan, and the creeping things, the worms, the dragons of the sea, and the creeping things of the deserts; and the Tora and Wisdom and Knowledge and Thought and the Gnosis of things above and the fear of heaven. Why dost thou reveal this to flesh and blood?

A:	FG:
Hast thou obtained authority from MAQOM? And again: Hast thou received permission? The Explicit Names went forth from before me	*I answered them: Because the Holy One, blessed be He, has given me authority, And furthermore, I have obtained permission from the high and exalted Throne, from which all the Explicit Names go forth*

with lightnings of fire and flaming chashmallim.

(9)*But they were not appeased, until the Holy One, blessed be He, rebuked them and drove them away with rebuke from before him, saying to them: "I delight in, and have set my love on, and have entrusted and committed unto Metatron, my Servant, alone, for he is One (unique) among all the children of heaven.*

(10)*And Metatron brought them out from his house of treasuries and committed them to Moses, and Moses to Joshua, and Joshua to the elders, and the elders to the prophets and the prophets to the men of the Great Synagogue, and the men of the Great Synagogue to Ezra and Ezra the Scribe to Hillel the elder, and Hillel the elder to R. Abbahu and R. Abbahu to R. Zera, and R. Zera to the men of faith, and the men of faith (committed them) to give warning and to heal by them all diseases that rage in the world, as it is written (Ex. 15:26): "If thou wilt diligently hearken to the voice of the Lord, thy God, and wilt do that which is right in his eyes, and wilt give ear to his commandments, and keep all his statutes, I will put none of the diseases upon thee, which I have put upon the Egyptians: for I am the Lord, that healeth thee".*

(Ended and finished. Praise be unto the Creator of the World.)

69025451R00120

Made in the USA
San Bernardino, CA
10 February 2018